PERFORMING ARTIST PATHWAY

NAVIGATE THE
HIGHS & LOWS
ON YOUR MUSIC JOURNEY

BRIANNA RUELAS

www.briannaruelasmusic.com

ISBN-13: 978-1979896061
ISBN-10: 1979896062

Victor. Gabriela. Gigi. Ruby.

You inspire me every day to grow, press on, make a difference, and reach my full potential. Thank you for loving me unconditionally and supporting all my "crazy ideas." Together, we can achieve anything. May we NEVER STOP DREAMING!

TABLE OF CONTENTS

INVITATION

Raise your hand if any of this sounds familiar:

Everyone around you has a talent, so you live your life comparing yourself to them, swimming in self-doubt and questioning the caliber of your own talent. You crave validation and rely on outside forces to fuel your confidence, while under-estimating the power of preparation and focus. You lack guidance and struggle to find the balance between practicality and creativity.

The path to discovering your place in today's increasingly competitive music landscape is no cake-walk. Face it—as an artist, you are a complicated creature!

Your journey as a performing artist is a tough one, chock-full of its own ups and downs—and why? Because you are wired differently. The artist has been inside of you since birth, and that will never change. You are who you are, and so you must find a way to stay sane and stable on your path . . . while also thriving and making a living! Being a creative is difficult, true, but there's more than meets the eye.

You can have all the training and technique in the world, but if you can't keep it together, when the going gets tough, it's all null and void. It is essential to address your emotional needs and have a balanced frame of mind in order to focus on the path before you and establish your own personal success.

This may be a bitter pill to swallow, but *you must change the way you operate, in order to fight your natural tendency of getting in your own way*!

As a performing artist, it is easy to become your own worst enemy. You are never satisfied; your talent and the work you create are never good enough. There is always something different you could have done or someone new to compare yourself to. But don't you worry: although you may feel as if you have nothing but problems, this book will teach you how to find your solutions.

Performing Artist Pathway: Navigate the Highs and Lows on Your Music Journey speaks to the real-life struggles you experience and offers solutions to support and encourage you along your journey. Honest and constructive, each chapter includes interactive sections that encourage you to ask the right questions, analyze your position, and challenge growth. *Performing Artist Pathway* will show you how to deliver your best audition and performance, promote your talents, and find true, lasting confidence. This book will also arm you against negative self-talk and teach you to overcome rejection and regret.

As a singer and performer for twenty-five years, I have studied internationally and performed all genres from jazz to rock to pop, received a BA in theatre arts from Pepperdine University, and spent years honing my musical theatre chops. While living the charmed performer life in Los Angeles for over ten years, I also pursued music and commercial voiceovers. I have fronted my own rock band and experienced the reality television craze in its early days as a Top 100 finalist on *American Idol, Season 4*.

PERFORMING ARTIST PATHWAY

I am passionate about encouraging others and can empathize with singers and performers, because I *lived* it. I know the frustration in giving everything you've got and *still* coming up short. I understand the range of emotions found between the pain of the "No" and the high of the "Yes!"—because I've been there.

Performing Artist Pathway will inspire the confidence to define yourself as an artist. In it, you will find the answers you need in order to make your journey the healthiest and most productive it can be. Through focus, discipline, and dedication, you will achieve your goals and create your own personal success story. This book will serve you not only in your life as a performer, but in your day-to-day world as well, because it teaches life skills applicable to your everyday.

I have seen tremendous growth among my students who have implemented the skills found in this book. Watching them learn the importance of "digging in," and as a result *thrive* as artists, brings me great satisfaction. My students learn the importance of marrying vocal technique and emotional connection, and are living proof that hard work—coupled with the right tools and focus—makes all the difference.

Performing Artist Pathway is that difference!

In this book, I promise support and encouragement along your music journey and a clear road map to navigating the ups, downs, and everything in between. *Performing Artist Pathway*, will help you gain the best competitive edge possible to bring you success. You will receive expert advice on everything from vocals and performance to style and self-promotion. You will define who you are as an artist, and then put your gifts to work! The tools you gain from *Performing Artist Pathway* will sharpen your skills and develop strength and confidence in your ability.

Do not expect instant change and greatness without putting forth any action. Do not allow sheer laziness or fear to assert priority in your life! Greatness reveals itself through challenge. When you introduce a new routine, you open yourself to discover something that did not exist. You have the potential to be a great performer, but you may never live up to that potential without allowing yourself the freedom to push through the discomfort. Be deliberate in your actions and *do the work*.

Perhaps the status quo is not working for you, and you're trying to sort out the Why? You need focus and change. You need accountability and an encourager. This book is for you! Make *Performing Artist Pathway* a book you start *TODAY!* Allow me the privilege of guiding you along your musical journey as I share my experience and expertise with you.

Over the years, I have created great relationships with experts in the industry who have given me tremendous respect for all areas of the business. Through my coaching—in addition to industry advice from talent agents, producers, stylists, mental trainers, singer/songwriters, musicians, and actors—*Performing Artist Pathway* will place you directly on a path to discovering your personal success.

Don't wait any longer!

Choose to become part of the solution and *dare to grow*!

1

How to Conduct a Personal Inventory

A re you growing as a performer, or just "comfortable"?

Each journey is different, but no one is exempt from the highs and lows that accompany life as a performer. Sometimes along our path we need a refresh. Taking the time to regroup and assess our current situation enables us to make the best possible decisions for ourselves. In the opening chapter of this book, I will guide you through the process of conducting a personal inventory and creating your very own "Artist State of the Union"!

Approximately every six months, I conduct my own personal inventory in which I take a long, hard look at my current life situation and determine my starting point. Through assessing your current situation you will uncover areas that need attention; this will promote spiritual, emotional, and creative well-being.

It's important to note that whether you're a beginner, a seasoned performer, or simply investigating, there is no right or wrong way to approach this inventory. Many of you may have no idea how to answer all of these questions, and that is absolutely OK. I encourage you to simply DO YOUR BEST!

For the questions that stump you, move on to the next. Don't drive yourself crazy, overanalyzing each question. This exercise promotes introspection and will help you determine your priorities and the desires of your heart. Your answers to the questions in this inventory today may be very different than your answers after reading this book!

There are many ways to approach your inventory, but I feel the best and most direct way to start is by answering a set of questions that begin with Where? What? Why? Who? When? and How? Below, you will find priority and follow-up questions. Start with the priorities, and then decide if you would like to take it a step further by answering the follow-ups.

As you are answering these questions, I highly recommend you record your thoughts, feelings, and ideas. Journaling is a great way to create awareness and put ideas in motion! As my gift to you, I have created a printable ebook, a *Performing Artist Pathway* companion notebook. By signing up at www.briannaruelasmusic.com/performing-artist-pathway you can have this notebook delivered straight to your inbox!

The companion notebook is dedicated to the growth and learning you gain from this book and can be used to answer the interactive questions after each chapter. Don't miss this opportunity! It only takes a moment to sign up at www.briannaruelasmusic.com/performing-artist-pathway and receive your FREE companion notebook!

Before answering the below, carve out time and space to be quiet and introspective. Only you know where you are most capable of getting in "the zone." Once there, open your notebook, put pen to paper, and let your words flow! Remove the self-judgment, take a deep breath, and *listen*. What are your heart and soul telling you? How do you truly feel? Don't be afraid to dig deep. You may uncover a pearl or two that's been hiding down there, just waiting to be discovered.

Priority Questions:

1. WHERE am I starting from? WHAT is my current life situation?

2. WHERE am I thriving and WHERE am I drowning?

3. WHAT do I want for myself?

4. WHAT are my challenges?

5. WHAT is good, bad, and ugly in my world?

6. WHAT actions do I need to take?

7. WHY do I want this? WHY have I chosen this journey?

8. Am I WHO I want to be?

9. WHEN is my next opportunity? HOW can I prepare for it?

10. HOW can I grow as an artist?

Follow-Up Questions: (for those who want to dig a little deeper)

1. WHAT is holding me back?

2. WHAT do I have the power to change?

3. WHAT junk or trash do I need to take out? Is there negativity I need to let go of?

4. WHERE can I say *no* in life, in order to create space for my priorities?

5. WHAT do I love about my life?

6.   WHO is on this journey with me who can offer support?

7.   WHO can hold me accountable?

8.   HOW am I doing, emotionally and spiritually?

9.   HOW can I improve my day-to-day life?

In this opening chapter, through conducting your own personal inventory, you assessed whether you are growing as a performer, or just "comfortable," and you identified your starting point. Don't stop here! Continue your journey and discover next the step-by-step process to achieving your goals.

We were created to be great. Push yourself beyond your limits of comfort and see how high you soar!

"The deepest secret is that life is not a process of discovery, but a process of creation. You are not discovering yourself, but creating yourself anew. Seek therefore, not to find out Who You Are, but seek to determine Who You Want to Be."

—Neale Donald Walsch

2

How to Put Your
Goals in Motion

Goals are very important when you're on the path to becoming who you want to be, but a plan of action—the steps you must take to reach those goals—is much more effective. But how do we create a plan of action? How do we set ourselves up for the best success possible?

In this chapter, you will learn about the three D's and the three P's and how they keep you on track, and finally how to write up your plan of action. By setting goals—and achieving those goals with your plan of action—you are taking the first step in making your desire your *reality*.

The Three D's and Three P's

Before you set your goals and create your plan of action, I would like to introduce a few amazing assets to utilize along the journey. This is not rocket science, but absolutely necessary as you navigate your path to success. I'll refer to these assets as the three D's and three P's.

The three D's are Desire, Determination, and Discipline. Desire is the want; Determination is the grit; Discipline is the action. Discipline is the anchor to the three D's and the most important of them all. Discipline encourages focus and clear intent and will keep you connected to your plan of action.

There are also a couple important bonus D's: Dedication and Drive. Dedication and Drive, coupled with Discipline, will answer the question, "How Bad Do You Want It?"

The next set of assets can be found through the three P's: Persistence, Perseverance, and Patience. Persistence is consistency; Perseverance is fight; Patience is love.

Don't miss the bonus, and equally poignant, P: Preparation. Preparation is the glue that connects the assets and fosters confidence.

Success does not happen overnight, so the three D's and three P's are essential to keeping you in the game when the going gets tough.

When My Going Got Tough: The Road to *Idol*

In 2004, I was in the midst of preparing for Season 4 of *American Idol*. I'd prepared for months, and my voice was in tip-top shape for the Las Vegas auditions. As to be expected for an *Idol* audition, on the day of I stood in line and waited for hours. When my opportunity to audition finally arrived, I stepped up proudly with my lime-green pants and sang my first song. The producer studied me and, with intrigue asked for another song.

After delivering my second, I saw confusion setting in.

"Do you have another?"

I had caught the producer's attention, but I wondered whether my third song would seal the deal. Unfortunately, my third song *wasn't* enough, and the letdown sunk into the pit of my stomach. My body went numb, and as I tried to process her words, spoken through a smile, "You were so close," I questioned what that even meant. Brokenhearted and dejected, I joined the thousands of other hopefuls who were turned away. Out of the approximate 10,000 who auditioned in Las Vegas that day, only twenty-four received their golden ticket to Hollywood.

I ached in the knowing that I was "so close" but came up short. After the Las Vegas rejection, I shut down, ignoring phone calls and invitations, and I disappeared. A month later, I felt ready to begin the healing process and finally emerged from my hermit shell. I received a phone call from my brother, who is one of my biggest supporters. "You know, Brie, I don't think you should stop. Are there any more audition cities?"

The three D's and three P's exploded in my mind—

Desire! Determination! Discipline!

Persistence! Perseverance! Patience!

—and as I listened, I knew my brother was right. My *Idol* story had just begun.

A few days later I packed my bags, hopped in Blanca, (my trusty white Ford Explorer Sport), and made the trek north from Los Angeles to San Francisco. On that six-hour drive, I felt the excitement bubble up inside me once again. This time would be different. I would take what I learned from my first miserable audition experience, grow from it, and approach the second audition with a fresh perspective. I was determined!

On audition day, I awoke at 3:45 a.m. and headed to Cow Palace. The lines were already wrapped around the parking lot, so I found my spot quickly and waited. If you have never heard the saying, "Hurry up and wait," this is what it's all about! Once in the arena, the Las Vegas memories flooded back in, and I fought to keep my insecurity at bay.

When they called my section, I felt like I was experiencing *déjà vu*. Once again, I was asked to sing three songs, and once again, on the last song I found myself in another staring competition with the line producer!

"C'mon," I shouted, "just give me a shot!"

I made the ask, and guess what? She said OK!

Persistence, perseverance, patience, and a little bit of luck paid off, and I progressed to the next round of auditions! In the chapters ahead, I will share more on my *Idol* story, and how you can gain from my experience.

Goal Setting and Plan of Action

Be flexible as you pursue your goals. There is not one cookie-cutter rule or path to follow. The journey to achieving our goals is different for everyone, and as life evolves we must modify the trajectory of our goals. By breaking up long-term goals into tangible, attainable short-term segments, you will be able to shift that trajectory when life calls for it.

In this chapter, you embraced the three D's and three P's and learned about goal setting and action plans. In your

Performing Artist Pathway companion notebook, answer the following questions and begin carving out your own personal plan of action. Don't be afraid to walk through this process multiple times in order to cover any short-term or long-term goals you may have. In the chapter ahead, you will discover how distractions knock you off your plan of action and how to avoid them.

Interactive Segment: Set Your Goals and Create Your Plan of Action

DATE:

GOAL:

Why do I want to achieve this goal?

Analyze My Position: Where am I starting this goal from?

Identify the Risks: List all the risks, REAL and IMAGINED, that I anticipate on my way to achieving this goal.

Identify the Obstacles: The obstacles on the way to achieving my goal are . . .

Identify the Investments and Sacrifices:

Identify the Additional Knowledge/Training that I will Require: List what I need to learn to accomplish my goal.

Identify the People whose Help I will Need: List groups, individuals, organizations whose help and cooperation I require to reach my goal, and the roles they will play.

Now Develop Your Plan of Action:

Everything I need to do to Achieve My Goal:

Activity	Priority Level	Target Date	Date Accomplished
1.			
2.			
3.			
4.			

How will I reward myself when all of this is accomplished?

3

How to Stick to Your Goals in a World Full of Distractions

This world is selfish and busy, and it's harder than ever to accomplish your workload! Distractions are deterrents that prevent us from finishing our work and ultimately reaching our goals. They can take form through people, technology, financial struggles, or even sheer arrogance.

In this chapter, you will create an awareness to the many types of distractions and learn how to keep from falling prey to their charms.

People and the Social Scene

Every day, you are bombarded by someone who needs something from you. Their intentions could be completely pure, or they could be a salesperson pitching some sort of good and/or service your way.

Be aware that people are distracting and can lead you on a wild goose chase if you let them!

Another way people become distractions, is through their invitations which clutter your social calendar with unnecessary events and commitments. Steer clear of the overly committed calendar, because you will inevitably become spread thin as you burn the candle wick at both ends. Take it from me—it's very difficult to be productive when you are stretched to your maximum.

Technology

Analyzing the amount of time you spend using technology is a great way to reveal whether you struggle with time management. The vortex of social media and the firestorm of text-messaging threads are major time-sucks and distractions.

When it's time to work, *work*!

You can always carve out time to peruse your Facebook or Instagram accounts. If you are in the thick of your focused work time, don't feel the need to answer each and every text or email immediately. Our culture demands information *now*, but for your own sanity and in respect of your art, I encourage you to fight culture on this.

Remove the technological distractions that interrupt your creative process!

Financial Struggles

Financial struggles are a very real challenge that can serve as a big distraction.

One reason pursuing a career in entertainment is difficult is because training does not come cheap. When money becomes a roadblock between you and your goals, instead of making excuses and halting your progress, find the best way to get around it. And if this section does not apply to you, be thankful for your opportunity and do not take it for granted. For the rest of you, read on:

When I was young, my parents could not afford the theatre classes and lessons I desired, nor could they afford to put me through college. Money was tight . . . but do you think my response was to simply give up? Heck no! My parents and I worked together to find a solution. The theatre company I attended granted me a scholarship, and it was there that I received the foundations of my training. I babysat and got my first "real" job in a pizzeria as a freshman in high school. I also joined my school choir and theatre programs and continued to grow. After high school, I put myself through college by applying for scholarships and grants and by working on campus. I found a way because I *prioritized* it.

Money becomes a distraction when we make it an excuse. Find a way! Don't ever blame money as the reason you don't pursue something important. If you value something and make it a priority, *you will make it work*. There are jobs to be had, products to be sold, and scholarships looking for a home.

Remember: there is always a way to make it happen for yourself.

Arrogance: The Big Fish in a Small Pond

Beware of becoming the big fish in a small pond. As the big fish you are an important player, yes, but only in a small sphere of influence. You can develop a stagnant mindset and even be filled with arrogance. Arrogance can distract us from creative growth; we become completely void of the ability to learn new skills; we ultimately waste our own time and never reach our potential. Choose to fight this distraction by challenging yourself to become the *small* fish in the *big* pond. Your ambition will allow you no choice but to venture out of your comfort zone, where new ideas and experiences are at your fingertips!

In this chapter, you took a deeper look into several popular distractions that deter you from reaching your goals. Whether people, technology, financial struggles, or arrogance are getting in the way, take a stand and prevent them from knocking you off the productivity wagon. Coming up, we will dive into the important balance our artist brains must establish in order to execute and achieve our dreams.

Now pull out your companion notebook for the interactive segment!

Interactive Segment:

Am I distracted? List the distractions that I am aware of and brainstorm realistic ways I can keep them at bay.

4

How to Balance Practicality and Creativity

In order to be successful as a performing artist, it is essential you engage the whole brain and balance creativity with practicality. When you choose to believe the myth that, because you are a creative artist, you are only right-brain dominant, you hold yourself back from achieving the fullness of your capabilities.

In this chapter, you will take a closer look into this brain myth, explore how creativity and practicality can coexist, and focus on why this balance is so important.

The Brain Myth

Growing up, I believed I was a right-brained person, because I was creative and artistic. This confused me, however, because in addition to being creative, I was also highly organized, which lends itself more to the analytical left brain. So how could I be both?

The truth is, the notion that from the left side comes logic and objective thinking and from the right side comes the more creative and abstract ideas, is a myth. Do not believe that because you are an artist, you cannot be logical, objective, and business savvy. A recent study, conducted by University of Utah's Director of fMRI Neurological Mapping Service, Dr. Jeffrey S. Anderson, concluded that there is no evidence of left- or right-brain dominance.

> "It is the connections among all the brain regions that enable humans to engage in both creative and analytical thinking."
>
> —Christopher Wanjek,
> Bad Medicine Columnist
> www.livescience.com

As an artist, you have the ability to use your whole brain to access creativity and use logic and objectiveness to respond with practicality. Practicality keeps creative folks productive, organized, and focused.

When Worlds Collide

Artists have a very natural tendency to live exclusively in their creative worlds. When the threat of practicality surfaces, tension grows. Producer and music director Austin Cope understands this tension all too well, and has discovered that as an artist he is not always considerate of others when it comes time to create.

> "I have something I have to get out! So even if I am mid-sentence with my wife, I have to stop everything I am doing to get whatever is in my head, OUT! My practical side fights with my emotional or creative side every day. I can't help it—I'm complicated."
>
> —Austin Cope

Be aware of protecting and respecting your relationships when the creative bug consumes you. Try your best to not allow others around you suffer in the name of your art! With this book project alone, I spent countless hours writing in the wee morning hours, after school pickups, and late at night. My children were amazing through the madness, but they suffered a bit while Mom lost her mind in creative la-la land!

The 85/15 Rule

Although, the two can butt heads at times, creativity and practicality can coexist harmoniously.

Time management is a great example of this. Carve out time for creativity and practicality by implementing the 85/15 Rule. Essentially, 85 percent of your energy will be spent in the creative zone, and the other 15 percent will keep you practical, on track, and focused. When you've exhausted your creativity, switch gears and focus that 85 percent on practical efforts.

As a performer, your creative zone may include journaling, songwriting, singing, acting, performing, and playing an instrument. Things you might do while in your practical zone involve research, characterization, memorization, vocalization, song dissection, and the emotion to real-life inventory (learn more on this in Chapter 10).

It's clear to see that without one it's hard to be successful in the other—both "zones" work hand in hand.

Let's explore a specific example of how the 85/15 Rule can work for someone preparing for a musical theatre performance. Your 85 percent may begin in the practical zone as you spend weeks memorizing and studying to become the character; you're vocalizing daily to build stamina and discovering authentic ways to connect to your character. As you're in this "practical zone," the 15 percent is getting creative through exploration; you might start dressing, eating and talking like the character. Once you have exhausted the research, it's time to switch gears in the 85 percent creative zone and become the character!

(A word of caution: your friends will think you are nuts!)

Another example of the 85/15 Rule is for the artist fronting a band as they prepare to rock the stage with a music performance. The practical zone is utilized in rehearsal, preparing for your set and promoting the event. Performance day arrives and it's time to turn it on and become a creative life-force! One artist notorious for "turning it on" is Beyoncé. Her creative life-force takes shape through her onstage personality, Sasha Fierce, and she "becomes" a different character, when she hits the stage.

For many artists, the thought of being organized or practical is the antithesis of productivity, because there's an assumption of restriction. I'm not suggesting you halt your process in the midst of a creative free flow, but tapping into the practical side of our brain—at the appropriate time—can aid us in staying focused and accomplishing more.

The Other Side of Practicality

Logic and organization are important pieces to your practical puzzle, but even more important are your basic human needs. This is a side of practicality that all artists and performers must pay attention to. You need to eat (including water) and have shelter and clothing. A very practical key to satisfying your basic human needs is, of course, money.

Supporting yourself on the road toward your dreams is another reason why balancing the practical and creative zones needs to be a priority. Unless you have someone footing the bill (lucky you!), you will need to find a way to pay the bills as you pursue your dreams. You can either find a job related to your industry or research odd jobs with flex hours. The blog Sonic Bids published a great article on "15 Unexpectedly Awesome Side Jobs for Musicians" which lists pet house sitting, tutoring, instruction, and even web development. For more ideas, check out: http://blog.sonicbids.com/15-unexpectedly-awesome-side-jobs-for-working-musicians.

A very common job for actors, singers, and performers needing flexibility is a job in the restaurant industry. I can personally speak to this experience, because I worked as a waitress and event coordinator for several years after college. (I even met my husband in the industry—and today we own a Dallas restaurant together!)

While working as a waitress, I recall a simple yet meaningful conversation I had with my grandfather. With his infinite wisdom he told me, "Every time you put that plate down on the table, smile and remember that the act of placing that plate in front of your customer is getting you one step closer to achieving your goal. Waiting tables is supporting your dream." My grandfather, with his analytical and brilliant mind, inspired me to continue working hard to support myself.

Before reading this chapter, you may have been among those who viewed practicality as a negative force in their creative process. Now, however, you can clearly see that when we create an 85/15 Rule (or even 90/10) for ourselves, we not only thrive creatively because we're more productive, but we also give ourselves a stronger avenue to supporting ourselves financially through our art. In our next chapter, we will focus on how to stay positive against a highly competitive environment.

Now get out that companion notebook!

Interactive Segment:

What odd jobs interest or make sense for me?

5

How to Stay Encouraged in a Dog-Eat-Dog World

The world and business of entertainment can be a cruel and harsh environment. It's easy to become discouraged by the staggering amount of talent seeking the same end result as your own.

When the statistics slam in your face, how do you stay positive?

In this chapter, you will find encouragement as you face fierce competition.

Remember your Why! When you are feeling defeated or frustrated, always go back to this. Remember why you're on this journey in the first place. A few chapters back, you put together a goals spreadsheet and plan of action for yourself. This activity was not created for you to tuck away in a drawer or bury under a pile of papers. Your plan of action was created intentionally and deliberately, to serve as a guide along your journey. Keep it handy for times of need and put it to use!

Stay Grounded

Stay grounded and confident in who you are and the greatness you are capable of. Surround yourself with people who authentically know you, love you, and want the best for you. If those in your inner circle are "keepin' it real," you will have no choice but to follow suit.

Have hope in difficult times and take comfort knowing that you don't always have to have all the answers. Believe in yourself and rely on this faith to keep you grounded. Maintain a fighting spirit, against negativity and tough statistics. There may be hundreds of thousands on the same journey as your own, but don't let this stop you!

During my second *Idol* audition, as I stood outside Cow Palace in San Francisco (in true cattle-call fashion), I tried to stay positive and refrain from sizing up my competition. I knew, however, what I was up against and that it would be no easy task, rising above the 10,000 *Idol* hopefuls. This was the last audition of Season 4, and the *Idol* producers had already auditioned approximately 90,000 singers! I was looking to be chosen among the .002 percent! Do you think I let that fact—that 100,000 people auditioned for Season 4 of *American Idol*—hinder me from giving my best? Of course not! I chose to stay grounded and focused, and to remember what I was there to accomplish.

Another way to stay grounded is by celebrating your mini victories and milestones along the way. I was seven years old when I earned a spot in the school talent show and, my big dream of becoming a star began. That talent show led to training at the Repertory Company Theatre, where I was molded and surrounded by encouragement. From there, I gained the confidence to audition for *The Mickey Mouse Club* and out of thousands of Dallas kids, I was a Top Ten finalist! (Fun side note: this was the season that Christina Aguilera, Britney Spears, and Justin Timberlake were on the show.) Perhaps I didn't make it on *The Mickey Mouse Club*—or become Mrs. Timberlake—but I celebrated the mini victory of getting so close.

Although life as a performer is full of competition, you can always choose to project light and positivity. Instead of becoming discouraged, allow it to propel you to be your best. Demonstrate to those around you the high caliber you are capable of achieving. You may not get everything in life, but in those times where you get so very close, grit is forming without you even knowing it.

In the next chapter, you will learn what it takes to define yourself as an artist!

> "There is nothing like a dream to create the future."
>
> —Victor Hugo, Les Misérables

Interactive Segment:

How do I stay grounded?

Make a list of my mini victories! However great or small, take the time to acknowledge how far I've come!

6

How to Define Who You Are as an Artist

Everyone has a signature sound, look, and style just waiting to be unleashed.

Defining who you are as an artist doesn't come easy for everyone. It can take years for many to truly tap into how we define our lane and identity in music. The "lane," or genre and style of music you choose, should feel natural and not forced; discovering this requires time and patience. In order to promote yourself—a topic you will cover in the chapter ahead—you must first determine who you want the world to see. This chapter is all about understanding and defining your Who? behind the artist.

When we define who we are at our core, it will translate into greatness in the area we are meant to be great in.

There is only one you! You are unique in your own way, and this knowledge facilitates power! Power gives you confidence to promote yourself and to perform at your best. When you are 100 percent confident in your own skin and in your own ability, that understanding is *GOLD!*

> "There is a vitality, a life force, an energy, a quickening that is translated through you into action, and because there is only one of you in all of time, this expression is unique. And if you block it, it will never exist through any other medium and it will be lost. The world will not have it."
>
> —Martha Graham to Agnes de Mille
> Martha: The Life and Work of Martha
> Graham – A Biography, by Agnes de Mille.

Discover Your Gold

Consider using a mind-map technique to discover more about yourself. To "mind map," you will need a blank piece of paper. In the center of the paper, write down your name. From there, offshoot with ideas or qualities that make up you! You can use descriptors and emotions like "singer," "upbeat," "confused," and include genres or even colors that represent you.

You can see below how my present-day mind map looks:

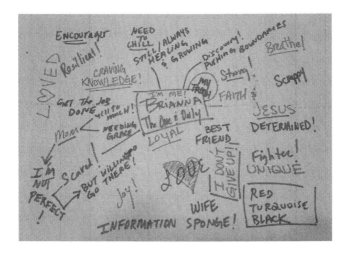

Another way to discover more depth is to dig into stories that have shaped your life, starting with your earliest memory—and be sure to include the highs and lows. Create a chronological timeline of events that have led to your present. Once the timeline is in place, expand on any poignant events by journaling, and uncover the life moments that spark emotion.

[WARNING: This may be painful, but defining WHO you are personally brings you one step closer to defining *you*, as the performing artist.]

Norman Matthew, international touring artist, producer, and owner of The Sound Foundation, gets to the heart of the correlation between personal growth and artist discovery:

"As a young aspiring artist, there are many steps along the way in your development. As you are evolving as an artist, you are also evolving as a human being. So don't try to be "the best" vocalist, guitarist, drummer, etc.

> Who decides this, anyway? Strive to be the best YOU! Kurt Cobain wasn't the best singer, Slash isn't the best guitarist—but theywere the BEST versions of themselves, and impacted the music world by being themselves on a thousand. And NO ONE can beat you at your own game. Don't chase your idols, simply wear them on your sleeve as a badge of honor as you travel on your journey to find yourself."
>
> —Norman Matthew

Don't Fight Your Sound

Have a clear understanding of your natural "sound." If you are on the fence between jazz and country, and your sound is twang and delight, strongly consider that your lane might be country. When I was auditioning for *American Idol*, Randy Jackson recognized the gravel and texture I have in my voice and likened my sound to Melissa Etheridge. Prior to that moment, I'd never considered that I could possibly sound like the rock star she is, but I was encouraged to work on some new material from her and dig into that genre a bit more. From that advice, I realized that my style is soulful rock. I may have pop and Texas influences, but soul and rock is my butter and jam.

Beware of the misconceptions of pop music. Pop music is defined as "music having wide appeal." Pop could be a lot of different genres, from rock to funk to soul. OneRepublic, Bruno Mars, Maroon 5, Kelly Clarkson, and P!nk are all defined as "pop" on iTunes—but there is so much more to these artists than the "bubble gum" material that some define as pop. Pop music is not confined to shallow lyrics and a strong hook. Pop can be layered, complicated, and full of depth.

Have you uncovered your "gold" yet? Whatever your lane is, embrace it. Thrive in it. Enjoy it! In the next chapter, you will pick up some powerful tips on how to show off your talent through self-promotion. (If you don't promote yourself, who will?)

Interactive Segment:

Create a Mind Map and Timeline Exercise to dive deeper into who I am as an artist.

7

How to Self-Promote Effectively

Once you have established a firm foundation in who you are an artist, it's time to start promoting yourself!

Remember: if you aren't going to promote yourself, who will?

By promoting your talents, strong work ethic, and gifts, you open yourself up to present and future opportunities. In this chapter, you will explore the most effective ways to self-promote. When you maximize the power of social media and utilize your networking skills, you increase your access to opportunity and brand-awareness.

Social Media

The number-one most effective way to grow your fan base is to promote online through social media.

If you are on the fence about who you are as an artist and the image you wish to convey, then STOP! Do not try to wing it! Once you open a social media account and start building followers, people will associate you with the content you post. It is crucial that your photos and videos are consistent and representative of you as an artist. Your image as an artist needs to be clear, cut and dry, with no room for interpretation. Know who you are before you present yourself to the world!

If you are still in the exploratory phase of your artistry, be patient and consider waiting to open your social media accounts. If you need a workaround, separate personal from business by creating one private account for friends and family, and (when you're ready) a separate public business account for all things music. There may be crossover of followers, because your friends and family will want to follow your music posts, but you can at least have a place to post private photos with family that the World Wide Web can't get their hands on.

There are a few tips that can help you grow your followers and help people find you when they are searching the World Wide Web. Facebook and Instagram ads are one way to promote yourself and increase an awareness of your brand. These ads can be targeted to specific demographics and markets and are very specific ways of growing your fan base. Engaging with your followers through commenting and "liking" posts also helps keep you at the forefront of their minds. The use of hashtags is another tool to gaining new fans. If someone is searching #music or #jazzmusic and your picture comes up, chances are they may explore your page further.

Social media offers insight through analytics that help you gain a grasp on who your audience is. Through analytics, you can find out where your largest group of followers live, and the days and times your posts receive the most attention. You can even spot trends in your posts to understand what photos and videos gain most attention. A selfie of yourself on the stage or a film set will most likely have more engagement than perhaps a picture you take solely of the stage or set. Statistics show that video tends to generate the highest level of engagement on social media. Discover what works best for you and stick to it.

Do the Research

Do your research and understand what social media platforms are available! Hootsuite conducted several partner studies among global users at the end of 2016 and concluded that social media is not only here to stay, but growing at a tremendous rate! They discovered that "2.8 billion were using social media at the end of 2016, up 21 percent from 2015. Mobile use increased by 30 percent year-over-year in 2016, surpassing 2.5 billion users globally (91 percent of all social media users)."

Against these statistics, it is hard to argue the viability of marketing and advertising on social media platforms. The engagement is present and globally active! Let's take a deeper look into Hootsuite's findings and narrow in on three major social media networks: Facebook, Instagram, and Twitter:

- Facebook is still the number one platform to consider for advertising, with, as Hootsuite says, "1.65 billion monthly active users and 1.09 billion daily active users. Fifty million businesses use Facebook pages" to promote and interact with their customers.

- Instagram is the "up-and-coming destination for advertisers," and the main reason is engagement. It is a rapidly growing platform and "has the highest per-follower engagement rate, 58 times more engagement per follower than Facebook." In addition, "Instagram users are 2.5 times more likely to click on ads than users on other social media platforms."

- Twitter, although highly popular, is primarily used to find up-to-date information and news happening around the globe. Although you can interact on Twitter, I don't believe it is the most effective platform for promotion. blog.hootsuite.com/social-media-statistics-for-social-media-managers/

Perception is Reality

In this day and age, the World Wide Web is king. People believe what they see! My good friend and actor Jason Faunt, best known as the Red Ranger from *Power Rangers Time Force*, has mastered the art of social media. In the early stages of Jason's acting career, he worked hard to show all of the exciting work he was doing. He created a perception of success, which later turned into his current reality.

"Show people how hardworking, dedicated, and excited you are about what you are doing in order to self-promote. When you are sharing your success with everyone and showing them how hard you are working, people will believe it and opportunities will follow."

—Jason Faunt

Today, Jason is a regular on the Power Ranger events circuit, where he has the opportunity to meet with fans and promote on all social media channels. Through a show he worked on fifteen years ago, Jason has maximized his earning potential—every month he receives passive income from it! He finds success through his 68,000 followers on Instagram, 19,000 on Twitter, and 72,000 on Facebook!

"Building fans and your following builds your brand and will create future opportunity.

And don't forget to hashtag!"

—Jason Faunt

Networking Inside Your Day-to-Day

Another way to self-promote is through networking inside and outside your immediate sphere of influence. It's as easy as simply opening your mouth and making an impression! Networking with friends and family can help propel your business forward.

Don't miss out on opportunities in your everyday world to tell people what you are up to! When I decided to quit my full-time job in advertising sales, it opened the door for me to explore my true passion of music and start my own vocal coaching business. I'm passionate about sharing my life experiences with those I mentor and coach, and making a difference in their life. I am an encourager. (A cheerleader at heart!)

When I first started vocal coaching and offering audition workshops, it was a slow process building my business. This all changed as soon as I opened up to friends and family around me, and they witnessed my authentic passion for my newfound career path. Simply sharing my excitement and networking with friends led to the growth of my vocal coaching business.

Cristal Givens, Music Business Entrepreneur and Owner of Alchemy Music, saw something in me that was different from the traditional vocal-teaching climate being offered in the Dallas area.

"There are times when the wheel needs to be re-created, or at least built upon. You were improving upon what I was seeing as the norm for vocal teaching. I think there is a difference between vocal teaching and vocal coaching. There is the "teaching" focus on technique and singing and then there is the "coaching," discovering depth found in the psychology behind it. You were teaching and coaching at the same time, while offering depth that I didn't see elsewhere."

—Cristal Givens

My relationship with Cristal is a perfect example of how networking within your circle can lead to the next career step. Cristal started as my neighbor. Fast-forward seven years, and she was hard at work toward opening a new music school in our hometown, and asked me to be a part of it! As a result of years building a friendship and keeping in touch, it led to an opportunity to work together. It also opened up a career path broader than I'd ever imagined!

Networking Outside Your Day-to-Day

Networking outside of your everyday world is another effective way to self-promote. The relationships you cultivate have the ability to create future opportunity.

As superficial as this may sound, "who you know" is a truth that pertains to all industries. Think about the steps you take when you need to find a job: you get the word out; you ask your parents, who in turn ask their friends; their friends may own businesses or have clients who they ask. The chain goes on and on, until you get hired! Network and talk to people outside your immediate social circle—and never underestimate the power of building solid and trusting relationships with new contacts.

Taking meetings, grabbing coffee, and attending events are all ways you can network and create new relationships. When I was in college, the Los Angeles entertainment scene was in my backyard. My father was on the creative end of commercial advertising in Dallas and introduced me to a few agents in Los Angeles. Again, it's all about who you know. I took the time to make phone calls and set up coffee meetings with them. I would ask advice and then follow up and keep in touch. Post-graduation, I went back to the agent I had gotten to know and gave him my voiceover demo in hopes to gain representation. I was fortunate and acquired representation from one of the top voiceover agencies at the time. I made the effort to network and develop a relationship with an agency, which over time, ended in opportunity.

Promoting yourself effectively in this busy and oversaturated world of talent is key to survival. In this chapter, you learned a few tips of the trade for managing your social media presence and the importance of opening your mouth—not just when you're singing!—and networking inside and outside of those in your life. Utilizing these avenues in a productive and responsible way will create opportunity.

Next up, you will dive into how to survive your love/hate relationship with music!

Interactive Segment:

Take out your companion notebook and get to work on these steps:

- Educate yourself further on best practices to promote on social media—and start with the platform that has the most engagement: Instagram!

- Schedule a few of your own coffee or lunch meetings and network! Write down at least three names of people to meet with—they can be friends, friends of friends, or work contacts.

- Research opportunities that will get you out of your comfort zone and networking outside your immediate sphere of influence.

8

How to Survive Your Love/Hate Relationship with Music

From a very young age, I've always loved music. It inspires me, restores my soul, and connects me with others. Music impacts lives . . . but despite the joy you feel from it, music can also be a source of frustration or sadness. A song can remind you of a painful memory, a failed or struggling relationship, or a missed opportunity or regret.

In this chapter, you will learn how to survive your love–hate relationship with music, through creating space, ignoring your stage in life, and diversifying your approach.

Give It Space

Similar to many relationships in life, sometimes you need to create a little space and breathing room between yourself and the thing you love. Space is the first way to survive your love–hate with music. Creativity is a living and breathing entity and has a way of becoming a nuisance. When you take time to give yourself space, you in turn take off the pressure, freshen up, and develop clear focus and direction.

Through the shifting seasons of life, your relationship with music may ebb and flow. You may court it for a few years and then break up. Eventually, if music is in your soul, your desire will start stirring and you will get the itch to reconnect. When you create a little space between yourself and music, you are able to return to it with a fresh approach.

Don't Get Hung Up on Your Stage of Life

Opportunities in your teens and twenties are different than in your latter years.

But who cares! What's age got to do with it anyway?

This perspective is another way to survive your love–hate relationship with music. Music is for all ages and stages! Don't dwell on the number. Despite the attention age receives, do not allow age to stop you from going after the things you want in life.

Age and life-experience can translate into wisdom. Today, in my late thirties, I appreciate who I am and have more confidence in myself. Through decades of singing and performing, I have learned the tools to take care of my voice and have developed my own, unique sound. Whether you are thirteen or forty, age does not define talent. Although the opportunities are different as we age, they can be equally exciting and fulfilling when you take on the right perspective.

> *"Life is not quantifiable in terms of age, but I suppose in my fifties I am more grounded and more at ease in my own skin than when I was younger. I have a confidence that I didn't have before from the experiences I've had."*
>
> **—Annie Lennox**

Diversify Your Approach to Music

My number one secret to surviving a love–hate relationship with music is to diversify your approach to it. When you diversify your approach to music, you wear many different creative hats. Wearing different hats is the same as exercising all of your unique talents and interests that pertain to music. Enjoy your creative season of singing and performing, and when that gets tiresome, take a break and pursue a different form of music, like songwriting or guitar. No matter the season or project, music is music, and your approach will feel fresh and exciting when you change things up.

One example of diversifying your approach to music can be found through my student, Mateo. Mateo is a fantastic multi-instrumentalist and vocalist. He is also an accomplished violinist; but as of late, he eats, sleeps, and breathes guitar. Mateo has the opportunity to sing rock music, play guitar and violin, participate in a vocal jazz ensemble, and lead musicians at his school. Although guitar is front and center for him today, I predict that one day in the not-so-distant future Mateo's love affair with violin will come surging back. Why? Simply because violin is part of his story as a musician.

In this chapter, you learned that through the ebbs and flows of life, music always exists. From singer to songwriter to musician and mentor, there is room for it all! When you diversify your approach to music, you allow yourself the freedom to connect with it, no matter the season of life you are in.

In the next chapter, you will face failure and discover how to rise above it.

Now let's open that companion notebook!

Interactive Segment:

List a few different ways I connect to music, to keep the love going.

9

How to Fight a
Failure Mentality

When we look at our lives and focus on all of the things we didn't or couldn't achieve, it's easy to feel like a failure. Shifting the energy to all you have accomplished—and all you will continue to accomplish—creates a much healthier mental perspective on life. In this chapter, you will redefine how you view "making it," examine the anomaly of luck, and ultimately take your stand against the failure mentality!

Have you ever heard the saying, "Those who can't, teach"? The actual quote comes from George Bernard Shaw's play, *Man and Superman*, and reads:

> *"He who can, does; he who cannot, teaches."*
>
> **—George Bernard Shaw, Man and Superman**

In this quote, Shaw expresses his opinion of the teaching profession as "second best." This quote had a very negative impact on me growing up, as I interpreted it to mean that if I couldn't "make it" on Broadway and ended up a teacher, I was a big, fat failure!

Growing up with this idea in my subconscious instilled fear. Mortified, I would think to myself, "If I don't make it, am I going to have to become a teacher?" In my teenage mind, becoming a teacher or a theatre director meant I had fallen short of my dreams because my talent wasn't good enough. I was conflicted by my terrible viewpoint, because in my mind I believed this lie, but in my heart I respected and loved my theatre director and all those who taught me.

When I compare how I felt about that saying at sixteen verses how I feel about it today, I still equally loathe it, because it immediately creates a negative connotation. Teaching is *not* failure, and I have found deep satisfaction through this career path. Singer, actress, and CEO of FireStarter Entertainment Talent Agency, Nicole Pryor Dernersesian, captures perfectly the importance of being open to evolving along your path:

> "Allow yourself to change. You get stuck when you don't allow yourself to be guided by your current interests. Don't get hung up on what you used to want. Trust yourself and don't allow the outside world to dictate what success is for you."
>
> —Nicole Pryor Dernersesian

What Does "Making It" Mean to You?

When you think of the phrase "making it," what comes to mind? Is it rising to the top of the entertainment ladder? Selling out mega-stadiums? Success, or "making it," does not happen overnight; instead, success is a culmination of years of experience, when all the right ingredients come together seamlessly. When you redefine your view of "making it," you can celebrate the highs and lows that have brought you to this place in life.

This very moment you are living today is a *success*! Just because your interests or original goal has changed doesn't mean you're a loser. Paths shift. Goals change. Don't let anyone tell you the "right" way to pursue music or define your path for you. There is no "right" way to do it. The only *right* is to pursue a path that is authentically you! Your experiences in life have brought you to where you are today.

You are a living success story!

Luck

One more way to take a stand against failure mentality is to accept that sometimes, talent has nothing to do with it. The entertainment business is part luck, part talent, and sometimes you just gotta be at the right place at the right time.

You'd be surprised how many singers and actors recognize that their talent wasn't all the reason they got to where they were going. In an incredible 2005 interview for *O Magazine* between Oprah and Charlize Theron, Theron brings to light how her lucky break came from a full-blown tantrum she threw inside a bank.

> *"I'd be unbelievably wrong to say there isn't such a thing as the right place, right time— luck. There are so many talented actors who don't ever get the chance."*
>
> *—Charlize Theron*

Read more at oprah.com/omagazine/oprah-interviews-charlize-theron/all.

Failure is a mental concept. Don't underestimate the power you hold to shift your mind's perspective on what this means to you.

In this chapter, you took a look at redefining what it means to "make it," and how you can take a stand against the failure mentality. You will never actualize your true calling if you're hung up in a negative space.

Next up, you will put any adverse thoughts behind you and explore clear and concrete ways to deliver your best audition!

Interactive Segment:

How do I currently define success and "making it"?

How can I take a stand against the failure mentality?

10

How to Rock Your Audition, Part One

W e've all been there before . . .

That panic we feel the night before an audition . . . we're cramming in our lyrics, learning last-minute melodies, and fighting the inevitable cold that accompanies stress! But we're hopeful our work at the final hour will actually help us to feel 100 percent confident and at our best.

Delivering a memorable and electric audition takes much more than remembering the words of a song. Preparation is essential in delivering your best. Part One of How to Rock Your Audition centers primarily on the singer/vocalist and covers four important steps you can take to rock your audition. Part Two, found ahead in

Chapter 12, will center on focus, visualization techniques, and making an impression in order to give you that added edge to rock your audition!

STEP ONE: THE BASICS

Confidence, developed through preparation, is key in delivering a successful audition. Below are five basic principles to consider as you prepare for audition day:

1. Know Where the Audition is Being Held.

Get the specifics! Time, date, location. Take responsibility and ownership of this information. Do not rely on friends, parents, or teachers for this. Be in the know!

2. Understand What They Require from You on Audition Day.

For musical theatre auditions, they are typically looking for 16–18 bars, or approximately a minute of music, either on a background track or piano accompaniment. If you are providing a track, have it either on a USB memory stick, CD, or, just in case, both! It's very unprofessional to expect whoever is casting to type in a YouTube link for you to sing with.

Lastly, for musical theatre auditions, be prepared to provide your résumé and headshot. Take pride in what you've done, no matter how little experience you have, and present yourself well. Make certain your headshot looks like you and represents *you* as the actor/singer/performer.

For all other genres or reality show auditions, have a clear understanding of what they're asking for. Determine whether you will need to provide a backing or karaoke track, accompaniment, or sing *a capella*. If you are required to provide a backing track, be sure to download one without backing vocals. If you're auditioning for a band, they will most likely give you an idea of the genre or song to prepare based on the type of band they are.

3. Spend Some Time with a Vocal Coach!

Preparing with a professional helps you determine your strengths and weaknesses, offers accountability, and can set you up for your best shot at success. A great coach will help you gain confidence in your identity as a vocalist and offer guidance on the best lane to showcase your ability. Hiring a coach you trust offers tremendous benefits which will serve you positively for years down the road.

4. Repetition Equates to Preparedness.

It is not always fun to drill information over and over, but sometimes that's what it takes to get the material down! Whether you work with a vocal coach, perform in front of a mirror, or do a mock audition with friends, practice makes perfect. When you neglect to put the work in to be truly prepared, you set yourself up for failure. You have to *want* it! When you put the hard work in, you demonstrate your *want* through action.

5. Have a Bag of Tricks.

Always be prepared with your "bag of tricks," so that when an opportunity arises, you are ready to deliver! If you don't already know what a bag of tricks is in this context, this is simply a reference to the songs you have in your back pocket, or songs you know you can execute flawlessly, at any given moment. Always have a minimum of three solid songs that are relevant to who you are as an artist.

STEP TWO: SONG CHOICE

Song choice is critical in an audition. By choosing the right song, you will convince the producer/casting director that they *must* cast you! Be sure to choose wisely; you'll need a song that best represents your talent, age, and range.

For musical theatre, they will either provide you with specific cuts or you will need to choose something unique and appropriate. If you are choosing your own material, find a song that mirrors the style of the musical you are auditioning for. If it's a classic musical like *Les Misérables* for example, don't choose a contemporary song from *Rent* or *Hamilton* as your audition piece. Go with something classic—perhaps *Phantom of the Opera*—and visa versa.

For those auditioning for record labels, television, or a band, choose something that is current and represents you as an artist. Casting directors want to know you are relatable to listeners today; they are looking for a fresh, unique sound. Up-tempo is preferred when it comes to television auditions—but if ballads are more your style, be compelling and have at least one up-tempo you can lean on.

Remember, you are in the world of entertainment . . . and people want to be entertained!

STEP THREE: SONG DISSECTION

Each time you work on a new song or audition piece, take the time to dissect it and pull it apart. Follow the steps outlined below, as you go through the process of song dissection.

1. Write Out the Lyrics!

Don't skip this! Although many of you have gone fully digital and rely on your electronic device to view lyrics, writing out your song lyrics can aid in the memorization process. Song dissection also requires you to write and take notes, so have your paper and pencil ready!

2. Listen to the Song and Mark Your Breaths (LISTEN, DON'T SING).

As you are listening to the song, start marking up your lyrics sheet with a pencil, where the natural breaths fall. I use a slash (/) to signify where the natural breaths need to occur, most often after each phrase; some use apostrophes. Do not underestimate the importance of breath, as it can make or break your audition!

3. Memorize Lyrics and Create Dynamics.

When a song is not memorized, the freedom of expression is difficult to create. It doesn't have to be perfect quite yet, but memorize as much of the material as possible. Add "color"—your personal flavor and vocal style—into the song. You have the ability to bring something highly authentic and unique to your performance, simply by being *you*!

Create dynamics to give your song movement and take your listener on a journey! (And if you aren't sure what dynamics are, ask your vocal coach.) If you start the song at a nine, on a scale of one to ten, you will have nowhere to go! Allow the song to gradually build in intensity, in order to make the strongest impact.

4. Character or Story Analysis.

No matter the genre you are auditioning for, it is important to understand the story you are trying to convey. Where does the story take place? What relationships impact the character? Knowing the details of the story helps create pictures and a deeper connection to the piece.

5. Work on Intonation/Connection.

Intonation is one way to capture the emotion or feeling of the song, and bring it to life. A great tool to aid you in this connection is the Emotion to Real Life Inventory (which you learn more about in Step Four coming up). By blending technique and intonation, you will deliver your best impact.

STEP FOUR: EMOTION TO REAL LIFE INVENTORY

In a performance, technique is dead when you lack the emotional connection and believability. As a singer, your vocal technique will only get you so far. You can sing pretty notes all day long—but if you don't evoke emotion, your performance will be forgettable and fall flat. When you succeed in emotionally moving your audience, you've accomplished your job. The Emotion to Real Life Inventory is a tool to help you create that personal connection.

Vocal technique and training is absolutely imperative, of course, but giving yourself the freedom to be emotionally vulnerable in your performance will facilitate connection to pain, happiness, excitement, or hope.

Coupling technique with intonation is the magic formula to rocking your audition!

I believe this is the difference between good singers and great singers. Great singers and performers understand the art of storytelling. When you demonstrate creativity in a raw and authentic fashion, you open the doors of communication and connection.

To conduct an Emotion to Real Life Inventory, identify the emotions found in the song and create personal mini stories that attach yourself to each emotion. This helps create an authentic connection to the material being performed. Relating to and then communicating a great story allows you to make it believable.

Emotion to Real Life Inventory

	HAPPY	SAD	ANGRY	CONFUSED
HIGH	elated excited ecstatic fired up	depressed disappointed hurt/alone hopeless	furious enraged irate seething	bewildered trapped desperated lost
MEDIUM	cheerful good hopeful relieved	heartbroken down regret distressed	upset frustrated annoyed disgusted	disorganized disoriented mixed-up foggy
MILD	glad satisfied mellow pleased	unhappy moody blue dissatisfied	perturbed uptight irritated touchy	unsure puzzled uncomfortable perplexed

	AFRAID	WEAK	STRONG	GUILTY
HIGH	terrified horrified petrified scared stiff	helpless hopeless overwhelmed exhausted	powerful aggressive forceful determined	sorrowful ashamed remorseful unworthy
MEDIUM	scared frightened threatened uneasy	dependent incapable tired rundown	energetic capable confident persuasive	sorry lowdown sneaky
MILD	apprehensive nervous unsure anxious	unsatisfied shaky lethargic inadequate	secure adequate capable able	embarrassed

In Part One of How to Rock Your Audition, you learned about the importance of preparation and connecting to the material you are performing. Preparation requires effort and commitment, but will set you apart on audition day.

To be certain your preparation is not in vain, it is important you address any fears or negativity that might be simmering. In the chapter ahead, we will address how to push through fear, negativity, and self-doubt to keep from sabotaging your own success.

Interactive Segment:

Create a personal Emotion to Real Life Inventory. Journal about personal stories, situations, or people that trigger feelings of LOVE, ANGER, FRUSTRATION, LONGING, HOPE, EXCITEMENT, THANKFUL-NESS, etc.

11

How to Avoid
Self-Sabotage

As a vocal coach, sometimes I feel like a shrink or a therapist without the formal training or ability to prescribe drugs. I work with artists every day—artists who experience creative blocks that hold their progress back. When you experience seasons in your life, when you are "off" or just down, many times the source of your pain is yourself.

Why do we sabotage our own success?

In this chapter, you will learn how to avoid self-sabotage by extinguishing fear, negative self-talk, and self-doubt.

Fear

Fear is the biggest way we sabotage our success—it is Enemy #1, the great robber of personal joy and satisfaction. Many people never get to the point of experiencing a new opportunity or audition, simply because they are too afraid. Fear of failure cripples action, inhibits progress, and essentially becomes a major roadblock to success.

You are not unique in your fear, as everyone has experienced it on some level. Taking risks and getting out of your comfort zone isn't a perfect process, so mistakes or even failure are inevitable. Acknowledge your fear, and then send it packing!

Don't allow fear to hold you back. There are more stories than I can count of entrepreneurs who have failed before they succeeded. Influentials like Spielberg, Lady Gaga, and Madonna all experienced failure and setbacks before becoming who they are today. They didn't allow fear to impede their overall opportunity for success—and neither should you!

The events in your life are stepping stones in life, and one event leads to the next. Overcome fear and open yourself up to receiving that "next step."

Nashville singer, hit songwriter, and 2015 BMI Song of the Year Winner, Heather Morgan, stares fear in the face on a daily basis:

"Anytime you are creating and putting something out into the world, fear is a real component of that process. Fear of being vulnerable or 'found out.' In my own creative life, songs are the words of my story, so putting my songs into the world is like putting my deepest emotions and memories into the air to be known. There is fear of how it will be received and whether it will come across as it was intended. Daring to create, in spite of fear, *is sometimes the battle you win first—and the rest is icing!"*

—Heather Morgan

Negative Self-Talk

As a performing artist, another way you sabotage your success is through negative self-talk. Negative self-talk is the actual expression of thoughts or feelings which are counter-productive and demotivating. Although there are useful ways to self-critique, if you are accustomed to negatively judging the sounds coming from your mouth, how will you ever grow as an artist? When you succumb to the doom of difficulty you've established in your mind, you limit your ability.

Internationally acclaimed voice-technique and performance coach, Steven Memel, understands the connection between our brain and body as it pertains to performance:

"Detach from your concept that something is difficult. The way your head conceives of things dramatically changes how your body does things. Neither making a pitch or forming a word by themselves, demands that you have to stretch your neck or reach. Therefore, you shouldn't have to stretch or reach, when you put them together. You must re-coordinate your muscles in order for them to function in more efficient ways. That means letting go of what you currently believe is working for you. If you're unwilling to let go, at least temporarily, of what you THINK is the "right sound," or "the right way to do things," you're essentially freezing yourself in time. The only way to achieve something different is to do something different."

—Steven Memel, LA's #1 Vocal Coach

(as voted by Backstage)

Negative self-talk is detrimental and completely the opposite of growth—so how do you turn this around? Start by asking yourself a few simple questions. Do you *really* believe you're a terrible singer or performer? Is there a deeper rooted problem that needs to be addressed? If the answer is yes, please take care of your mental and emotional health by consulting with family and a professional counselor. If the answer is no, most likely you are struggling with insecurity.

Many times, negative self-talk is a symptom of insecurity and is no easy issue to battle. First, acknowledge and become aware of how and when you allow it to show up in your life. Awareness is usually the first step to creating change. Focus on creating a positive self-image and commit to ending the harsh self-judgment. Insecurity is very common, and you may need support to overcome it. There is no shame in talking to someone to get the support you need. Having the tools to assume a healthier mental perspective can make all the difference.

Another aspect of negative self-talk is something called "imposter syndrome." This is the idea that you don't deserve your success, despite proof you are highly competent, which in turn drives you to live in fear of being exposed as a "fraud." Many successful artists and entrepreneurs—including myself!—have experienced this; if you have ever felt this way, you're not alone! Trust yourself and your ability, and remember: you gotta start somewhere!

Self-Doubt

Self-doubt is another roadblock you create for yourself. When you lack confidence in your ability and emphasize the *I Can't*s in your world, you say goodbye to progress and growth. Focus on TRUTH to battle self-doubt and squash the "I Can't Complex."

The TRUTH is, you are skinny enough and you are beautifully made.

The TRUTH is, you are interesting and unique, and no one else has your story.

The TRUTH is, your voice is terrific!

Visually focus on your truth and start believing it! There are times in life when self-doubt will creep in quietly and permeate her darkness throughout your mind. It is never too late to snuff out her darkness and replace it with light. Journaling your strengths, gifts, and truth can serve as a reminder of who you are at your core.

There is a *reason* you are on this journey.

> "I praise you, for I am fearfully and wonderfully made. Wonderful are your works; my soul knows it very well."
>
> —Psalm 139:14

Another way to combat self-doubt is to positively value your worth. Instead of "I Can't," shift to a solution-oriented perspective like, "This is a challenge . . . how can I tackle it?" Accept the challenge and put the work in. Don't expect to see different results when you lack the action to change the status quo.

In this chapter, you learned how to fight fear, negative self-talk, and self-doubt in order to avoid self-sabotage. This awareness will open you up to your truth and give you confidence in an industry full of ups and downs.

Get out of your own way, and prepare for take off!

Coming up, in Part Two of How to Rock Your Audition, you will examine the roles *focus* and *visualization* play in setting you up to achieve your best.

Interactive Segment:

To battle fear, negative self-talk, self-doubt, journal my truth and record my strengths and gifts.

12

How to Rock Your Audition, Part Two

Prior to audition day, preparation is necessary for success—but there's additional action you must execute in order to bring forth your best.

In Part Two of How to Rock Your Audition, you will learn the importance of focus, visualization technique, and making an impression in order to give you that added edge to rock your audition!

Focus: The Horse Stable Theory

When I was twenty years old, I had a conversation with my grandfather that still impacts me to this day.

He made a very simplistic idea extremely relevant as he told me a story about the horse stable he built on his property outside of San Diego. "Before I built this horse stable, I had to visualize it in my mind. I had to see it. You too must do the same."

Through focus, see in your mind exactly what you want and execute it. My grandfather's Horse Stable Theory is applicable to all areas of life and is a great tool for focus along your journey.

The environment around you can play a large role in adversely affecting your focus. In an audition, you could either be performing next to a loud room, full of hopefuls trying to get their big break, or in a cold, dry auditorium with bad acoustics. Always do your best and do not allow circumstance to shake your confidence.

Don't waste your time playing "the game." The game is when you start comparing yourself to the room full of people you're auditioning against. When we play this game, we deplete our focus and our energy shifts in a negative way. Whether intentional or not, everyone sizes each other up at auditions. Focus instead on what you are there to accomplish.

You are there to deliver your best, shine your light, and slay your song!

Get out of everyone else's business and worry about your own.

Battling Nerves or Stage Jitters

Nerves are a very natural part of the audition experience, but you must train your brain to not let them get the best of you. Many times, pre-audition jitters take place due to a lack of preparation and focus. A simple reminder to yourself that you are prepared will translate into the confidence you need to keep nerves at bay.

Another way to battle nerves is through breathing and visualization techniques. Mental trainer and retired Air Force Master Sargeant Gaetano Fedele is trained to work with high performers.

"Visualization is a way to mentally rehearse the actions associated with your audition or performance. The key, when you visualize, is to not resort to a negative past or future performance with a poor ending. You cannot control what people watching you think, so why be anxious about it? Ultimately, stay away from the past and future thoughts that can sabotage your hard work. If you find yourself thinking in the past or future, take a couple of deeps breaths and reset your focus."

—Gaetano Fedele

Make an Impression!

Making an impression at an audition starts the moment you step foot in the room. Show your personality and charm, combined with professionalism and responsibility. *Slate,* a term from film which means saying your name and the material you are performing. Stand tall with shoulders back and a strong posture. Smile and exude confidence. The director not only wants to cast talent, but they also want to cast someone who is easy to work with!

Let there be no doubt that you are happy to be there and eager to learn and grow.

Dress to impress and be memorable! Wearing something memorable really paid off for me at the final *Idol* callback in San Francisco. As I got closer to my audition time before Randy, Paula, and Simon, I caught the eye of one of the producers. "Lime pants!" she said. I was shocked to run into the *"you're so close"* line producer who hadn't put me through in Las Vegas! She remembered me, though—and those lime-green pants definitely helped! She looked me dead in the eyes and said, "Don't let me down. Show them you belong here." And boy, did I! Following our exchange, I received my golden ticket to Hollywood.

Make your dress age appropriate and relevant to the genre you are in. Do not arrive to an audition looking sloppy. Consider the role you are auditioning for and avoid costumes or trying to dress like the character. You want casting to see *you*, not your costume. Consider an outfit or accessory that helps you stand out and sets you apart! It's very possible that you could be remembered as the "flower-dress girl," the "fohawk dude," or even in my case, "the lime-green-pants girl."

Prior to your audition, think on how you might answer the question, "Tell me about yourself?" or "What experience do you have?" Present your response with confidence and make it interesting. Casting directors are not asking your name—they're trying to get an idea of who you are. Have the courage to *show* them your personality. Communicate that you want to be heard and seen—and *never* apologize at the top of your audition with, "I'm sick." As harsh as it may sound, no one cares that you've been sick. Simply do your best with what you have to work with that day.

Through focus, visualization, and making a strong impression, you now have the tools to put your best foot forward. Take confidence knowing you will leave it all on the stage and that you've given 110 percent. Once you do your part, the rest is in the hands of casting.

In the chapter ahead, you will dive deeper into the world of casting and how to keep yourself from going crazy trying to control the process.

Interactive Segment:

What does my "horse stable" look like? Journal the WHO, WHAT, and WHERE I want to be. Don't leave out the specific details that fully paint the picture.

13

How to Find Peace with the World of Casting

Wouldn't it be nice if you could read minds and know exactly what someone wants?

This would be very helpful in an audition scenario where you really want a specific part and the only thing coming between you and that role is the casting director on the other side!

Don't make yourself crazy over-analyzing what they were looking for. The fact of the matter is, what they're looking for can change at any moment and you must find peace in the uncertainty. In this chapter, we will explore the many factors that are taken into account when casting decisions are made.

As Julia Roberts was coming off her award-winning role as Erin Brockovich, she pitched to director Steven Soderbergh her desire to play a "dark and emotionless" role in his upcoming dark tale on drug trade, *Traffic*. But Soderbergh would have nothing of it. In a 2000 *Entertainment Weekly* article, senior editor Josh Wolk captures Soderbergh's rational perfectly:

> " 'I said, "It would require you to extinguish everything that I find compelling about you," ' remembers Soderbergh. 'It's unimaginable to me to cast her [in a somber] role, when her gift is her life-force that really makes you want to watch.' "
>
> ew.com/article/2000/03/22/why-steven-soderbergh-turned-down-julia-roberts-role/

Casting is not personal in nature—it's business. Despite her talent and box-office pull, Soderbergh knew Roberts was not right for the *Traffic* role. He had business to conduct and needed to get the right players in place for his next epic.

Talent

Any time a director is casting a show, they have their unique ideas on how the show should come together. Whether they are casting for a musical, a television production, or a new lead singer in a band, whoever is casting typically has a good idea of the look and sound they are going for. Although it is always possible that an audition can inspire new ideas for the director, in most cases, a performer should trust the director's vision and not fight it.

As the performer, the only thing you have control over is yourself. The best thing you can do is show up and present to them your best. An important and, many times, *difficult* idea to accept is that you could be the most talented singer in that room, but your best may not be enough. You might have all the talent in the world, but if you aren't right for the part, very rarely will it go to you.

Talent only takes you so far.

"Everybody has talent. Talent means virtually nothing. It's not about your talent, but more about how hard you are willing to push and work to do something with it. There are plenty of talented people who never do anything with it. Be easy to work with, have a great attitude, hustle, and deliver."

—Adam Pickrell, multi-record producer

Social Media Presence

Chapter 7 covered the importance of self-promotion and building your online presence. Today, more than ever, social media is taken into account in many casting opportunities. It's very common nowadays to receive the question, "What social media platforms are you on and how many followers do you have?"

To provide an example, think of two people auditioning for the same role. One has 200 followers and the other 20,000. There is a strong chance the opportunity will go to the person with 20,000, simply because of their fan following. Unfair? Perhaps. But the casting director knows that 20,000 fans and followers can be accessed when it comes time to promote their project.

Educate yourself through the wealth of resources available on the internet on how to boost your social media statistics. You can also hire a professional to help you out—unless you prefer having that personal touch with your followers.

Either way, there is no harm in asking for help if you need it!

There will always be a new and improved platform to promote on, but one that I believe is here to stay is Instagram. To learn more on leveraging your reach, check out the online Instagram course with Dean Street Society. Learn more at deanstreetsociety.com.

Typecasting

Typecasting is still very present in our current entertainment landscape, and it involves more than simply what you look like.

Typecasting is defined as "assigning [a performer] repeatedly to the same type of role, as a result of the appropriateness of their appearance or previous success in such roles."

Typecasting could be based on anything from the color of your hair or skin to the demeanor of your personality. With that said, there are many productions and casting directors going against the mold and casting outside the predictable confines of how the character/part typically "looks."

Casting directors are not immune to making mistakes from time to time. Mistakes can be made when they are trying to rush the process or determine the cast too quickly. Perhaps a callback was needed, but they didn't have room in the schedule for one. The first time I was hired as a music director for a musical production, I made this great mistake.

We were up against the clock and needed to cast the show quickly before end-of-year finals and summer break. I felt rushed to make my casting decisions and didn't fully think through the choices made. As a result, there was one very key actress who missed out on the lead role. Instead, she was cast in the ensemble and went on to become my assistant music director. I believe a callback would have remedied this casting mistake.

Another way casting directors make mistakes is when they choose "type" over "talent." Sometimes, casting directors are so focused on casting someone who "looks" the role that they overlook the performer's ability to execute it. By choosing the performer who has the necessary talent, who may not exactly fit the "type," casting can rest assured they have a compelling production on their hands.

Audition for every opportunity that comes your way! Say yes and don't try to talk yourself out of it or analyze whether they will cast you. Don't worry about whether you think you are "right" or "wrong" for the part. You never know when a past audition of yours will prompt a call today with the perfect opportunity!

In this chapter, you gained perspective on how to find peace in the casting process. In the grand scheme of things, one audition leads to the next and it truly is a numbers game. Coming up, you will learn how to unlock your confidence when performance time arrives!

Now pull out that companion notebook!

Interactive Segment:

If I were going to be type cast, what opportunities would I be considered for?

14

How to Unlock Confidence with Every Performance

Y OU GOT THE GIG!!!

. . . now what?

The work has just begun. I urge you to *not* be that singer who believes now is the time to relax. The very opposite is true—now is the time to kick it into high gear and show them what you're made of! Whether you're the lead, a supporting cast member, or rocking out with a band on a live stage, you will need the skills learned in audition-prep Chapters 10 and 12 to make an impact and deliver your most confident performance!

In this chapter, you will receive tips on rehearsal and building a connection, stage and performance day advice, guidance on pushing through nerves, and style recommendations.

I know ... sounds overwhelming, right? Don't worry. Let's dive in!

Tips for Rehearsal

We perform like we practice, as they say; therefore training and repetition are key to confidence.

Rehearsal is critical, no matter what genre you're singing. You learned all about focus and visualization in the previous chapter, and now is the time to put those tools to use once again. Think about your horse stable. Your performance is just one more step to get you there. Take advantage of the opportunity you've been given, visualize yourself on stage, and rehearse as if it's a live performance every time.

Your attire and the way you dress during a rehearsal can also impact how you move and focus in a performance. Dress appropriately. Imagine showing up to a rehearsal wearing flip flops, sweatpants, and a hoodie. How can you expect to channel your character or work the stage in flip flops? This type of attire inhibits performance and can hold you back.

Show up to rehearsal *ready to move*.

Connection

As a performer, accessing stories from your Emotion to Real Life Inventory (see Chapter 10) will give you the confidence you to need to connect in a personal and meaningful way. Before you even begin singing the song, associate it with memories or stories that connect you to the material. Remember: just because you didn't write the song doesn't mean you can't build an authentic connection to it.

One way to connect is through keeping your chin directed to the audience, acknowledging those onstage with you, and not performing to the ground. Don't spend the entire time on stage with your back to the audience or in your own world. Your own world is probably very nice, but the audience would like to be a part of it as well.

Your fans want to get to know you! Let them see who you are, understand your process, and feel how the music impacts you. Whether you have one, five, or hundreds of people (or *thousands*!) coming to see you, give them a show! Share the story of your character, the music, and the lyrics by opening your eyes and letting them see your heart. Through breaking the fourth wall, you give your audience the opportunity to build an authentic connection.

One of your important roles as a performer is to stir people's hearts in a way that makes them feel alive. Whether they're crying, laughing, dancing, or experiencing a sense of peace, you have the great privilege of facilitating authentic emotion. Don't strip away that access by getting so caught up in your own world that you forget to connect.

Game Day Routine

Having your plan laid out on performance day is another way to unlock confidence. Establish a routine that will help you relax and enjoy your upcoming time onstage. Try starting off your game day with "wake, stretch, and run." Stretching and cardio put me in a positive, clear frame of mind and also warms up my vocal chords in the process. Exercise also translates into energy and promotes breath stamina. Another benefit is that exercise makes you feel physically strong, which translates to mentally feeling good. This gives you added confidence.

Avoiding stressful situations on game day and finding ways to relax is a crucial practice. A nice jog serves as great tension relief to keep stress from taking a toll on your singing voice. Another relaxation method can come through a hot steam shower, which also doubles as a great place to vocalize.

Yelling at those around you because you aren't prepared or stressed is *not* helpful!

Not only will it deplete your creative energy and positivity, but it also makes everyone around you miserable (not to mention unwilling to work with you again).

A few hours before your performance, work through your material and refresh to reinforce muscle memory. But don't overdo it! You've prepared up to this point and can take confidence in that.

Avoid caffeine, carbonation, alcohol, and decongestants leading up to a performance. All of these impact your voice and most allergy medicines completely dehydrate you, placing major stress on your vocal chords. If you suffer from allergies or have a cold, find a way to homeopathically reduce the symptoms or visit your ENT (Ear, Nose & Throat doctor) to find an alternative medication that won't dry you out.

Leading up to your performance, hydrate throughout the day sufficiently with water. Proper hydration increases the natural mucus coating our vocal folds need to prevent friction caused when singing. Although you can certainly sing without being adequately hydrated, the chances of you being at your best are slim.

BRIANNA RUELAS

Even with a well-hydrated body, you may still complain of having a dry mouth. New York based Vocal Coach Dan Parilis explains this:

> "Though water does hydrate and eventually moisturize the vocal folds, it does not really stimulate the salivary glands, which serves to moisten the mouth and lubricate the vocal folds at the moment one drinks it."
>
> —Dan Parilis, Vocal Brilliance
>
> vocalbrilliance.com/vocal-hygiene-part-2-hydrate-hydrate-hydrate-why-hydration-is-important-to-singing/

Eating or drinking saliva-stimulating foods like apples, apple juice, or pineapple juice can help combat dry mouth. Although pineapple juice sounds like an odd choice, it might be what saves you from blowing out your voice due to overcompensation. (Another product I really enjoy is Mouth Kote Dry Mouth Spray.)

125

Combatting Nerves

In order to personify confidence, it's imperative to conquer those nerves! Nerves are a very natural way our body reacts to stressful, exciting, or new situations. They may start off as a flutter in your stomach, but if you're not careful they can blow up into a paralyzing predicament! Find a way to convert your nervous, pre-performance energy into focus and control. When you look uncomfortable on stage, it's because you are uncomfortable inside! Recall your visualization techniques (learned in Chapter 12) and put them into practice.

The preparation and rehearsal time you have invested leading up to this performance have prepared you for this moment. Whoever gave you this opportunity gave it to you because they *believed* in you! Now is the time for you to believe in yourself. Do not withhold your talent and energy; deliver the goods, get out of your head, and let go of the negative self-talk.

You *CAN* and you *WILL* do this!

Performance Style

Image, style, and dress play a major role in shaping our confidence on performance day. Stylist, talent manager, and *Rock Family* TV creator Tiffany Forsberg recruits and works with young talent every day. Forsberg notes that most young people ages 13–18 today have a definitive idea of their image or how they want to dress, but Forsberg feels there are certain things that look better on stage and boundaries on clothing to watch for.

"With young women, don't wear anything too provocative. For example, short shorts, bras, and high heels. For filming, avoid shiny clothes, as they catch light. Other don'ts when filming would be don't wear white and don't wear loud prints. Avoid too many band T-shirts, so that the focus can be solely on the music. If you're a band, you don't have to match exactly, but have a theme and allow *your look to go together. Most of the time, with styling, the performer's confidence receives a boost because they feel and look good on stage. Looking put together will give you more confidence and therefore result in a better performance on stage—plus, your fans will love it!"*

—Tiffany Forsberg

Performing with confidence communicates strength and captivates fans!

In this chapter, you learned how to unlock your confidence through tips on rehearsal and connection, stage and performance-day advice, conquering nerves, and style. All of these work together to position yourself to rock your performance! In the chapter ahead, we will address a topic very close to my heart: depression and how to battle the blues.

But first—that companion notebook!

Interactive Segment:

What gives me confidence?

Do I practice like I perform? If not, how can I fix it?

Create my own game day routine.

15

How to Press On When Depression Hits

It's natural to get bogged down with heaviness when life crashes out of our control.

When depression takes hold outside of our "plan," it can be very difficult to stay focused. How do we continue our creative process, or even perform, when the storms of life hit? How do we keep it together when painful events occur in our lives, bringing us to our knees? Whether it's heartbreak, traumatic loss, divorce, a physical or emotional challenge, or even financial stress, real life has highs and lows.

In this chapter, you will create an awareness of how to press on through the dark days of life and find healing in the creative process.

In my early twenties, I fell in love. My personality has always been one that loves deeply, falls hard, and doesn't hold back. When I commit, I am 100 percent *in* and as loyal as they come. I thought this relationship was "the one," but after a year, it abruptly ended. "Crushed" doesn't even begin to cover how I felt during that time. I had a voiceover commitment in Hollywood the day I received the news. As I entered the studio, I fell apart. A blubbering mess, I couldn't function, and ultimately had to walk away from the job.

Like the romantic I am, I kept thinking this guy just "needed a break," and would realize the amazing woman he was walking away from. This false hope only opened me up to greater hurt three months down the road when I experienced betrayal for the first time. My ex had started a relationship with someone I thought was my close friend from work. (She broke the "girl code.") I spent a year mourning that failed relationship and my art was virtually non-existent.

Don't let this happen to you! My top advice for combatting depression is to seek professional counseling. Counseling equips you with tools to rebuild, in addition to a safe environment to heal. Seek out support to get you through your lowest of lows. Yes, broken relationships are painful, but they are not the end of the world. Life does go on, and I wish I would have gotten the professional support I needed during that difficult time.

A great starting point as you begin to heal is to meet your challenge head on. Get to the root of the problem and discover the best solution for navigating the pain. Tend to your wounds. When you experience trauma, unfortunately, you may never forget what happened, as the experience becomes part of your story; nonetheless, find the strength to put one foot in front of the other.

As artists, there's an opportunity to take our pain and suffering and allow something beautiful to come from it. Create the space to feel and acknowledge your emotion and experience it. If you choose to simply sweep all of your problems, worries, and "junk" under the rug, pretending it doesn't exist, you create Band-Aids to conceal the pain and don't actually heal.

Don't miss your opportunity to authentically connect with yourself and others who may be experiencing something similar. With time, you will find hope and strength to turn your pain into creative gold that impacts and inspires—through the power of music.

Beware of Performance Addiction

Performing can become a great Band-Aid to help us forget about our current pain.

Beware of performance addiction.

I liken it to an addiction to drugs or anything that gives us a high. We crave the praise and attention performing brings us, and when we don't receive it, we crash—*hard*. We step on a slippery slope and seek performance opportunities for all the wrong reasons. We also try to live up to the world's—or even our own—standards of "perfection."

Beware of placing your value in the wrong things. Wrapping your worth solely in your identity as a singer can lead down a very dark and insecure path.

When life throws punches, first and foremost, know that you are not alone. Support is only an email, text, or phone call away. You were never promised that life would be easy or fair, and at the end of the day, the only thing you have control over is your perspective and attitude. Depression is painful, but get the support you need, and do your best to not allow the debilitating nature of depression consume you forever.

In the next chapter, we will explore the final tough topic, very real for anyone on this journey: rejection and regret.

Time to break out that companion notebook!

Interactive Segment:

Do I need support through a dark season of life? Who can I talk to? (Please highly consider researching a list of professionals to go see.)

Write down 2–3 people I can receive support from and include at least one professional.

16

How to Let Go of Regret Caused by Rejection

Rejection is a difficult pill to swallow on your journey as a performing artist. The disappointment and regret experienced after days, months, even *years* of that perpetual "No" take their toll. To survive, one must develop very thick skin, as rejection is part of the entertainment game. In this chapter, you will gain perspective on how to let go of regret caused by rejection's painful sting.

When you protect yourself from potential pain of rejection by pretending you don't care about an audition, you set yourself up for defeat before you've even had the chance to perform. Talking yourself down in order to keep your expectations low promotes a defeatist mentality and cynacism does not encourage a stellar performance or audition.

Consider the opposite approach. What if, instead, you positively built yourself up with, "I've got this!" Approach your audition with the best attitude possible, present your best performance, and hope for the best outcome. No matter how many times you don't get the part, or receive that dreaded "No," or hear "You're not right," always enter an audition with a positive energy and outlook. When you rest in the confidence of knowing you did your best, regret loses its grip simply because your performance is not in question.

Another way to let go of the regret accompanied with rejection is by understanding that, many times, the outcome of your audition has nothing to do with your talent or ability. Singer/actress and CEO of FireStarter Entertainment talent agency, Nicole Pryor Dernersesian, is often asked by her clients if she received any feedback on *why* they didn't get a certain part. The true nature of the entertainment business is revealed, as Dernersesian very simply states:

> *"The feedback is, you did not get the part.*
> *They have gone in a different direction."*
>
> *—Nicole Pryor Dernersesian*

My *Idol* Regret

As important as it is to let go of regret, it's still part of life. Even if you believe that everything happens for a reason, regret can still find a way to slip into your subconscious. It's as simple as looking back on something you wish you could've handled a little better.

In this section, I will share with you one experience in particular I wish I could've handled a lot better. My big regret stems from when I blew my *American Idol* audition during the Hollywood round.

I had been preparing for months, had an exercise routine in place, and was working with renowned Los Angeles vocal coach Steven Memel. I felt strong mentally and physically and my confidence was sky high. On the day I got my golden ticket from Randy, Paula, and Simon, one of the things Randy kept saying was that he loved the rasp in my voice and that it was "very Melissa Etheridge." My song choice was a bit inconsistent, so they wanted to see more of that soulful, rock vibe from me. Naturally, I took the judges' suggestions to heart and began preparing my best Etheridge material.

In the two-month span between receiving my golden ticket and the Hollywood round, I moved apartments. Forgetting to notify *Idol* of my move was my first mistake in a string of unfortunate events leading to the most horrible audition of my career.

[Insert dramatic *"Dun dun dunnn."*]

A week prior to the Hollywood round, I noticed I hadn't received any information on the audition. I called the offices immediately to check in and discovered they'd mailed my packet to my old address. Yowza!

I rushed to the *American Idol* offices in Hollywood that afternoon to grab my packet. (Fortunately, I lived in LA at the time and was able to do that.) To my shock and dismay, there was a CD inside the packet with strict instructions to choose two songs from the ten provided. Out of the ten songs, the closest thing to "rock" was "The Letter" by The Box Tops. I chose one more—"Ain't No Mountain High Enough" by Marvin Gaye and Tammi Terrell. All of the time and money I'd invested working my Etheridge material with LA's top vocal coach Steven Memel was completely in vain. Well, not completely, because he's still my vocal coach—and my mentor as well!

Distraught, I set out to learn, polish, and connect to the new material in one week's time. Neither song I chose felt "right" for me, but out of the ten these were my best options.

I didn't have the cash to schedule another vocal lesson with Steven, so I tried to prepare on my own.

This was mistake number two.

For such an important opportunity, I should have found a way to work in one more vocal lesson. In addition to polishing the material, Steven could've also provided valuable input on song choice, as this was not my strong suit.

The day arrived and I made the two-hour drive, fifteen miles over the hill to Hollywood. I recall meeting Adam Lambert briefly and thinking, *Now HE looks like a rock guy!* There was also another Brianna auditioning who had blue hair. The game was on, as I started comparing myself to the other rockers. *Idol* was casting a show, after all, and they needed to fit all their different characters into their neat, perfect squares. As much as I wanted to fit in one of their squares, I knew deep down I was a "divergent": a music mush-pot full of soul, rock, jazz, and Texas.

In our run-through with the music director and accompanist, she informed us of a change in the arrangement for "Ain't No Mountain"; the music break between verses was removed. As we listened to the changes, I struggled with focus and was knocked off my game, leading to fatal mistake number three.

What came next was mortifying.

It was finally my turn to shine and I entered the stage with confidence. My first song was "The Letter," which should have been sung a few steps higher, so it lacked energy and fell flat. I had one more chance to "wow" the judges with "Ain't No Mountain," but to say I missed the mark is an understatement. This song came across as the *antithesis* of "wow"!

I completely forgot the revised arrangement, and when the second verse started in I paused for the nonexistent music break. The piano continued while the hundred other contestants stared at me from the audience seats. Randy, Paula, and Simon looked confused, going back and forth between the piano and my hot mess. I'll never forget Simon's disappointed face, which communicated, "This is pure rubbish!"

The judges were justified in their disappointment. I was a complete waste of their time that day. "Rubbish" is a great word for how bad I blew my audition, and I am very aware of the mistakes I made. Singing "The Letter" felt forced, and I missed an opportunity to truly make it my own and memorable. In addition to missing the changes in arrangement, "Ain't No Mountain High Enough" was not the best song choice for me either.

The beauty in looking back on this disappointing memory is the wealth of knowledge I gained from it. As they say, hindsight is 20/20. I learned humility, resilience, grit, and perseverance. I can look back and actually laugh over how terrible I performed that day.

Instead of grieving the failure and living in the past, I'm truly thankful I had the opportunity in the first place.

Allow this chapter to help you accept rejection with grace and let go of regret. The next chapter is a little different and speaks to the loved ones in your life supporting you on the journey—specifically, your parents. Pass this book along to them, but don't skip it! There's value in it for you, as well!

> *"When one door of happiness closes, another opens; but often we look so long at the closed door that we do not see the one which has been opened for us."*
>
> *—Helen Keller*

Interactive Segment:

Learn from your mistakes! Ask yourself the following questions after each audition or performance, and record them in your companion notebook:

1. What can I do differently next time?

2. What can I learn from this situation, this audition, this performance?

17

How to Support the Artist in Your Life

M any of the parents I work with have have been thrust into a "brave new world." First and foremost, they tell me, they have no idea what they're doing or how their child got the performance gene in the first place. That may be, but supporting your child in a positive and healthy way is of the utmost importance.

In this chapter, you will receive my three pearls of high-level advice on how you can support your own young performing artist as they embark on their music journey!

Hire an Expert

I have the privilege of coaching students of all ages and stages, and receive questions every day from parents who don't know what to do with their young, aspiring performer.

My first suggestion is to hire an expert. Whether it's a vocal coach, acting coach, or artist mentor, bring someone on board to support your efforts.

Many parents make the mistake of assuming they can coach their child because they watch *The Voice* each season. You might be a lover of music and know what is appealing to the ear, but if you're not an expert in vocals, do not try to coach your child on his/her singing technique. Leave that to the coach whom you have hired to guide and train your child.

Out of meddling comes bad habits. Be their parent, not their coach.

I consider myself an expert in my field and have three young singers in my household. Even as an expert, I hired a vocal coach for my oldest—because she needs me to be her mom, not her vocal coach. I impatiently wait for her to ask me for guidance instead of my offering unsolicited advice every time she opens her mouth to sing. I'm all business when it comes to coaching; my direct, honest approach makes my daughter feel like I'm picking on her. When the same advice comes from someone else, it's amazing how she responds and applies the information.

Know When to Give Feedback or Support

Think about your first response after you watch your child's performance. Do you go straight to the critique and remind them of what went wrong? Do you praise them for the good job and give them a high five? Or somewhere in between? Know your child and whether they truly want your honest opinion or simply a pat on the back.

I advise to wait until they ask you, "What did you think?" Waiting for this question could take hours or days, but once it comes you can respond to the effect of, "Do you want encouragement or do you really want to *hear* what I have to say?"

Most artists are well aware when they've had a rough show, and simply need a hug or smile of support from you. I find that most performers prefer to hear constructive criticism from their vocal coach or mentor rather than from their parent.

Don't feel like you have to offer your opinion or loaded critique after every performance. I see both ends of the spectrum—from militant to cheerleader—when it comes to parenting styles. If you are more "militant" in your style, you set high expectations, expect nothing but the best, and guide with tough love. If this is you, your approach may work beautifully—but don't forget that your artist needs affection and a little soft encouragement from time to time!

On the flip side, if you have the "cheerleader" style of parenting, you are a super encourager, not an expert in performance, and have figurative pom-poms waiting in your purse to bust out at any given moment. If you are the "cheerleader" parent, I recommend openly communicating to your child that you're their number-one fan, but that you're not an expert. This is not to devalue your opinion of their work, but your artist needs to understand that just because Mom said "Amazing job!" doesn't mean their performance was unflawed.

Get Out of the Way

My last bit of advice to you is to get out of the way!

Let your artist drive the train. Their desire to grow, excel, and pursue auditions and opportunities needs to be *their* desire—not yours. When accompanying them at auditions, don't spend the majority of your time kissing up to the casting director. You may think you are pleasant, but in reality you're causing your child more harm than good.

You could have the most talented kid in town, but no one wants to work with a pushy parent or the child of a pushy parent. Take it from talent agent and CEO of FireStarter Entertainment, Nicole Pryor Dernersesian, who has clients in New York, Los Angeles, Las Vegas, and everywhere in between. Dernersesian has let go of clients, not because of the child's talent, but because of the parent's behavior.

> *"Despite how talented your kid is, or how much money there is to be made, I cannot work with a parent who is out of line. Life is too short to deal with crazy people, especially when a child is involved."*
>
> **—Nicole Pryor Dernersesian**

Get out of the way—let your artist shine and do their work! This will serve them better down the road. You are not doing them any favors in the long run when you hover over every move. Yes, connect them and create opportunities if you are able—but once you get them there, allow them to pave the road for themselves. You only set them up for disaster when you make them dependent on you. Your child will be an adult soon, and will need to stand on their own two feet.

For many of you, that day has already come, and so it's time to let go of the control. As my favorite inspirational author Ellen Miller would say, "Let go of the kite!"

"By trying to mold the ones you love into what you want them to be, you're only setting yourself up for frustration and an exhausted heart!"

—Ellen Miller,
The One Year Book of Inspiration for Girlfriends . . . Juggling Not-So-Perfect, Often-Crazy, But Gloriously Real Lives

Are you growing yet? Or still just "comfortable"?

Either way, you've reached the end of your journey with me, for now. I hope *Performing Artist Pathway* has provided you the tools you need to refresh, focus, dig deep, embrace the journey, and create your own success as a performing artist. This is only the beginning, and it's up to you to keep the momentum moving forward.

Challenge yourself to grow and realize your potential!

BONUS CHAPTER

Expert Advice

*P*erforming Artist Pathway is chock-full of helpful advice and wisdom to accompany you on your music journey. Throughout the book, in addition to hearing directly form me, you also learned a few things from a few of my industry pals. As industry experts, ranging from stylists to producers to singer/songwriters and talent agents, their insight is invaluable to your education as a performer.

This bonus chapter is like the extra scene that takes place after the movie credits roll, and is my sweet gift to you for making it to the end of the book! Don't miss the Acknowledgments section at the end of this book in order to learn more about the experts you've met in these pages.

Enjoy!

DO THE WORK!

Do not expect results without doing the precious work of educating and getting to know yourself. In *Performing Artist Pathway*, I create an interactive opportunity to dig in and journal after each chapter. If you haven't received your **FREE** Companion Notebook, complimenting the interactive sections, sign up now at **www.briannaruelasmusic.com/performing-artist-pathway!** For anyone who opposes the idea of journaling, let me encourage you to push outside your comfort zone and do it anyway. This is a crucial step on your journey to discovering who you are, what you want, and how to get it!

THINK ABOUT THE LONG GAME
STEVEN MEMEL

Los Angeles' acclaimed voice-technique and performance coach Steven Memel speaks on the importance of having longevity and tenacity in the entertainment business:

"Don't expect success overnight. Think of your career as a long game. People will say no to you, but no can mean, 'No, not right now!' Don't get hung up on 'I blew my chance.' Instead recognize that they have to know WHO you are, in order to say no to you! That is the beginning of a relationship. Now it's up to you to nuture that relationship and gradually shift that 'no' to a 'YES!' They will watch as you keep up-leveling your skills and eventually, you'll get so good they just can't ignore you!" Ultimately, in the long game, you will get a yes from them, because you will maintain the relationship in a positive way, and they will see your growth! You must last it out until your skills are at a level where they can't ignore you!"

—Steven Memel

FIND A PERFORMANCE COACH!

Whether you're a vocalist, musician, or actor/actress, increase your skill level by including a performance coach as part of your team. Find a coach you trust who will challenge you and give you the tools to maximize your ability. As a singer and vocal coach, even *I* need a vocal coach! Steven Memel is the best coach I've ever worked with. He was voted two out of the past three years as Los Angeles' Number One Vocal Coach by *Backstage*, and has coached stars like Adam Levine, Sara Bareilles, and Halsey, to name a few—not to mention me!

Through my work with Steven and watching him work with others, I have witnessed results with my own eyes and experienced them personally. I not only experienced growth in my performance, but the tools he has given me to strengthen my vocal muscles and extend my range, enable me to hit notes I never thought I was capable of hitting. Working with Steven gave me the confidence to approach difficult material and make it simple for myself.

VOCAL EXERCISES

Vocal exercises were not created for you to execute perfectly onstage. You do not have to "sound good" when singing your exercises. There are many purposes behind vocal exercises that can range from simply warming up the muscles to "working them out"—that's why their called exercises! Compare vocal exercises with pumping iron to strengthen the body. When you perform bicep curls and bench presses regularly, you strengthen your muscles and develop stamina. If you stop going to the gym and performing these exercises, your muscles will decline and eventually atrophy. The same is true with your vocal muscles . . . which is why I stress the importance of keeping them in shape!

Don't be afraid to use unconventional methods to challenge your vocal muscles as you step out of your comfort zone. Engage your vocal muscles in different activities to promote healthy vocal growth. Exercises might feel weird or strange and you may feel uncomfortable and make mistakes. Get of of your head, release the fear, and allow yourself to make mistakes. It's

OK to sound "terrible." You won't ever learn if you're striving for perfection all of the time, so just go for it!

As in life, when we get out our comfort zone and push ourselves, we open ourselves up to reaching our potential and becoming the fullness of who we are. I find the same is true when we break out of our comfort zone as a singer. Exploring the innumerous ways our voice can make sound, however odd or "normal," can ultimately pull out the best we have!

EDUCATION
NORMAN MATTHEW

Take advantage of any opportunity to learn and grow. From dance lessons to improv or performance coaching, don't get too comfortable. Always continue educating yourself!

Singer/songwriter, producer, and owner of The Sound Foundation, Norman Matthew, offers his insight on education:

> *"Educate yourself. An educated musician will be the empowered musician. Especially in this day and age with the new music business model and the power to have your career in your hands as an independent artist. You need to take control, know what it is you are taking control of, and maintain your controlling interest in your dream. There is no better way to fight the fight than understanding that this is called 'music business,' not 'music friends.' "*
>
> *—Norman Matthew*

ON SOCIAL MEDIA
AMBER LAFRANCE

As covered in Chapter 7 on Self-Promotion, social media is a crucial avenue of marketing to master. Music publicist and brand strategist, Amber LaFrance, has a very specific formula she advises her clients on:

> *"Create the four pillars of what make you uniquely you. If it is not you, don't post it. If you have a young demo, they will probably never look at your website except through your phone, which is why social media is so powerful."*
>
> **—Amber LaFrance**

KNOW YOUR VOCAL LIMITATIONS

As a vocalist, understand your physical limitations when rehearsing and performing. Many times, artists will push themselves past their limit, beyond exhaustion. When you rehearse tired, you put yourself in a precarious position to potentially harm your voice. Excessive use can even lead to vocal nodules or permanent damage of your singing voice. Overcompensating to get the sound out, creates strain and unnecessary tension. I highly recommend that you never push when you are tired. Know when to take a break and give it a rest.

PUNCTUALITY AND PROFESSIONALISM

As a performer, it is crucial that you value professionalism. When you commit to a show or gig, do your best to overcome all obstacles and honor your commitment. Unless you're laid out with a 104° fever, no cold or inconvenient allergy symptom should ever keep you from a performance.

The show must go on!

You do not want the reputation as a performer of bailing out on performances at the last minute. Make adjustments if possible and commit to pushing through your performance, despite any physical challenge you may be experiencing. Don't assume defeat before you've even begun. Acknowledge you are not physically at your best, and then simply *do* your best. The show is counting on you!

Remember that preparedness and punctuality are important components of professionalism. Arrive on time—which is actually *EARLY*! Allow yourself enough time to set up your gear and get into performance mode.

BE BUSINESS MINDED
CRISTAL GIVENS

Music business entrepreneur and owner of Alchemy Music, Cristal Givens, stresses the importance of understanding the business side of your craft:

"Think like a brand and treat your music career as a business, from the beginning."

On your brand . . . "Be a good steward of your brand. You are your own best advocate and your brand is how others perceive you. In this digital age, it is all about perception and your brand can have a history tracing back to your first social media account."

On business . . . "Debating whether to go to college? — There is no question; a business degree is a solid investment. However, no matter what, you are forever a student of business. Always be reading, learning and broadening your knowledge through network-

ing, workshops, meet-ups, online courses and good old trial and error. Cultivating your mind for business will serve you and help you become more successful, in all you do."

—Cristal Givens

FIND A MENTOR!

Having someone who can offer guidance—and someone who has been around the block a few times—to support your journey is invaluable.

You don't always have to "know it all." You are not born with all the knowledge and answers you need. Over time, when you seek it, you grow in wisdom and knowledge. And here's a little secret: you can have more than one mentor to support the different aspects of your life and business. Connect with a mentor who resonates with your purpose and path, and keep pressing as you encourage and impact lives!

PERSPECTIVE ON SUCCESS
JASON FAUNT

Actor Jason Faunt has been appearing in film and television for seventeen years. What many do not know is that he is also a successful financial planner for a major firm. Jason has a great perspective on success and how it translates into confidence:

> *"Years after my big break, I am still working as an actor and I'm very happy with my place in life. I celebrate my mini successes and social media helps me maximize each opportunity. When you analyze your levels of success appropriately and gain perspective, this will help you take hold of your confidence."*
>
> *—Jason Faunt*

EXPLORE NEW MUSIC

One thing that makes a great singer is understanding great music, no matter what the genre or decade. Be well rounded in your knowledge of all genres of music, including the oldies and the newbies. You don't ever want anyone to discredit what you can bring to the table because you don't know who Freddie Mercury, Otis Redding, or Gladys Knight and The Pips are.

(But seriously, if you don't know who these artists are, do some homework!)

Experience live performances as much as possible. Pay attention to how an artist performs onstage and how they interact with their audience. There are always lessons to learn from each show you see, whether it's something you *should* or *shouldn't* do. When you witness different performers and genres, you open yourself up to creative inspiration, because by listening to different performances we trigger a different creative experience and response.

SEEKING TALENT AGENT REPRESENTATION
NICOLE PRYOR DERNERSESIAN

Singer, actress, and CEO of FireStarter Entertainment talent agency, Nicole Pryor Dernersesian, speaks on how to know when you're ready for talent representation:

"You know when you know. First, consult with a professional or a vocal coach and be honest when asking yourself, 'Do I have enough talent? Do I have what it takes?' An adult should have a full résumé if they are seeking representation. If the potential client is a child, I start with the kid and see how interested they are. Immediately following, I interrogate the parent and ask them if THEY are ready! In many situations, the parent must

quit their full-time job to have flexibility and cater to their child's audition and performance schedule. It is ultimately their job to become the educator and create a sense of normalcy for their child."

—Nicole Pryor Dernersesian

EXERCISE YOUR CREATIVITY

Creativity can be accessed through inward reflection and shared through emotional expression. It is important to carve out time to be creative. When we calendar this time in, we use a very practical method to organize our creative chaos. Don't always wait for the inspiration; instead, train your brain to flex your creative muscles.

In writing or journaling, for example, when you commit to engaging your writing muscle thirty minutes a day you create a productive habit. Over time, you improve your writing skills and accessing your creativity becomes easier.

To grow creatively, diversify your sources of inspiration. Draw from music, art, film, and even nature. You could be on a walk or run and suddenly something triggers a great song idea or fresh approach to an idea or character you are playing. I've discovered that most of my wild ideas surface when I'm either outside in nature, in my shower, or "between sleep and awake in Never-Neverland."

SONGWRITING
HEATHER MORGAN

Take it from Nashville hit songwriter, Heather Morgan, who writes for country stars like Keith Urban, Brett Eldredge, and Kenny Chesney, to name a few:

"One thing I've learned by being around so many songwriters my whole career is that we all have something we do that is unique to us. These days when I listen to the radio, I can guess who wrote a song based on hearing something in a song that stands out—it might be a melody or phrasing or the idea as a whole. The more you write, the more you find what those unique qualities are, those personal touches that make our songs ours. We all have them—we just have to write and find them."

—Heather Morgan

TIPS WHEN SINGING WITH A BAND

If you're a vocalist, know what key your songs should be sung in and how to communicate the tempo. Musicians who work with vocalist will often choose the singer who knows how to speak "musician language" over ones who don't—any day of the week. Challenge yourself to learn music theory, so you can perfectly understand your lead sheets. A great resource to get you started on this can be found at musicnotes.com/blog/2015/07/16/lead-sheets/. There are also apps like irealpro.com that can help you establish the correct key for all the songs you sing.

ON STYLE
TIFFANY FORSBERG

You don't have to break the bank to define your style as an artist!

Stylist, talent manager, and creator of *Rock Family* TV, Tiffany Forsberg, speaks to finding signature pieces on a budget:

> "At the end of the day it comes down to the music, but style plays a major role in creating confidence on stage. I like to hit thrift stores and sites like Etsy to find cool and unique things that you aren't going to find everywhere. I also shop inexpensive stores like H&M and Forever21."
>
> —Tiffany Forsberg

ADVICE FOR THE STUDIO
ADAM PICKRELL

Multi-record producer Adam Pickrell gives his expert advice on attitude when working with producers in studio:

"When you are going into a session, hang your privilege at the door. No one cares to deal with anyone who has a big ego. You are going in to do a job. It is an equal playing field when you enter the studio, and you are no better and no worse than anyone else in that room. If you are playing ego games, you have no business being there and need to leave."

—Adam Pickrell

For singer/songwriters entering the studio for the first time to record original music, I absolutely love the warning Pickrell provides below:

"Remember first that you hired a producer. You're not there to tell them what to do. If you already know exactly what needs to happen, than don't hire a producer. The quickest way to get a bad rap is to hire a great producer and then not listen to a word they say. You'd be better off just hiring an engineer to do what you ask, rather then waste a producer's time."

—Adam Pickrell

WITH GRATITUDE

There are so many friends and family that have supported my journey—through the ups, downs, and everything in between. To you all, I am eternally grateful.

Thank you to Mom, Dad, Wendy, Skae, Anthony, and Guy, for always cheering me on. Thank you to the women in my life who make up my "Village." To my Mastermind Ladies and my Launch Team, who support my efforts to share *Performing Artist Pathway* with the world!

A special thank you to all my students, who are the muses behind *Performing Artist Pathway*.

To my friends and industry experts: Austin Cope, Nicole Pryor Dernersesian, Jason Faunt, Tiffany Forsberg, Gaetano Fedele, Cristal Givens, Amber LaFrance, Heather Morgan, Norman Matthews, Steven Memel, and

Adam Pickrell. I am grateful you have chosen to be a part of this journey with me and sincerely thank you for your time, wisdom, and participation!

ABOUT THE AUTHOR

Brianna has a passion for music and understands talent. As a singer and performer for twenty-five years, Brianna has studied internationally and performed all genres, from jazz to rock to pop, received a BA in theatre arts from Pepperdine University, and spent years honing her musical theatre chops. While pursuing music in Los Angeles, she also worked as a commercial voiceover actor. Brianna has fronted her own rock band and experienced the reality television craze in its early days, as a Top 100 finalist on *American Idol, Season 4*. Currently, as a vocal coach and artist mentor, she focusses on private vocal and performance coaching, mentoring and group workshops.

Brianna is a Dallas based, singer/songwriter, vocal coach, and artist mentor. She is a proud Wife and Mother to three girls, Creator of Every Mom's Story Blog and works alongside her husband, to keep their family restaurant, Victor Hugo's thriving.

Brianna is currently booking workshops, speaking engagements, and is available for coaching and mentoring via Skype. Follow Brianna on social media @briannaruelasmusic or contact her at briannaruelasmusic.com/contact/.

INDUSTRY EXPERT BIOS

Austin Cope: Music Director and Producer

Austin is a producer and musician born and raised in Dallas, Texas. He owns his own studio and has been making music his full-time career since 2008 as a producer, studio musician, and music director.

Nicole   Pryor   Dernersesian: Talent Agent/Singer/Songwriter/Actor/CEO of Firestarter Entertainment

Nicole was born a performer! Typical of her incredible work ethic, she studied classical voice at Pepperdine University and graduated with a degree in advertising and music in only three and a half years. In September 2012, after six and a half years and over 2,600 shows with the Las Vegas Company of *The Phantom of the Opera*, Nicole transitioned her company, Firestarter Entertainment, established back in 2008, into a fully registered and bonded talent agency. FSE has grown exponentially from year to year and now has over 600 clients from coast to coast.

Jason Faunt: Actor and Social Media Expert

Jason is no stranger to film and television, but he is known most notably as the Red Ranger in *Power Rangers Time Force* and the motion-capture for Leon Kennedy in the *Resident Evil* franchise. Through his experience as an actor, he has developed an incredible knack for connecting with his fans through all social media platforms. He will be reappearing in the upcoming installment of *Power Rangers* in 2018.

Gaetano Fedele: Mental Trainer

Gaetano earned his masters degree in psychology with an emphasis in sport psychology from Capella University. During an impressive twenty-one-year Air Force career,

Gaetano performed, led, and mentored Airmen to meet mission requirements in no-fail situations. His military experience provided insight into the importance of remaining calm under pressure, having confidence in your training and abilities, staying focused on the objective, and being both mentally and physically prepared to perform. As a certified mental trainer, Gaetano fuses his military experience, mental training skills, and sport experience to assist athletes and performers of all types with developing the skillset needed to perform in "The Zone." Gaetano enjoys distance running, coaching youth sports, and working with performers and competitive athletes in all sports. Gaetano is based in Dallas and provides services globally via Skype.

Tiffany Forsberg: Talent Manager, TV Producer, Stylist

Dallas-based producer, stylist, and talent manager, Tiffany Forsberg shares her experience as a stylist and image consultant for young performers. With over seventeen years as a model and stylist, she works with celebrity clients and has many magazine tear sheets under her belt. She knows how to create a look that will get you noticed and fit your image. "The minute I meet an artist and hear their music, I've already picked out the look in my head."

Cristal Givens: Music Business Entrepreneur and Owner, Alchemy Music

Cristal has always had a passion for music and an entrepreneurial spirit. Immediately out of high school, she began working at Sound Warehouse, interning with PGD and various indie labels and distributors while attending community college. Within four years, she was running her own grass-roots music marketing company, working with artists and labels such as Ani DiFranco's Righteous Babe, Capricorn Records, Pointblank Records, Blue Thumb Records, and Osmose Productions. In addition to twelve-plus years in music marketing, she has over fifteen years in traditional digital marketing, including co-ownership in the digital agency, Content

Pilot. She now heads the operations of Alchemy Music, a new concept music school and talent development program she launched in 2014; as of January 2017, she is the director of the PCG Universal Dallas office; and as of October 2017, she teaches the Business of Music at MediaTech Institute Dallas campus.

Amber LaFrance: Music Publicist, Brand Strategist, and President of CultureHype

"PR maven Amber LaFrance is making a name for Dallas artists." —*Dallas Observer*

Hardworking, diligent, and passionate about her clients, she thrives off of working with creative brands and like-minded people. A music-obsessed marketing guru, Amber started her own creative marketing and PR firm in 2011, CultureHype, and became a full-time entrepreneur. She's spent the last five years working local, regional, and international press campaigns and loves supporting emerging artists. An advocate for Dallas visionaries, Amber has made it her mission to shine a spotlight on North Texas arts and culture.

Norman Matthews: Singer/Songwriter/Multi-Instrumentalist, Producer and Owner of The Sound Foundation Music School

Born and raised in El Paso, TX, and now living in Dallas, RIAA award winner Norman Matthew cut his teeth by hitting the road at the tender age of sixteen, chasing a dream and perfecting his craft. This road led to touring with rock luminaries such as Rob Zombie, Korn, The Used, Deftones, Five Finger Death Punch, The Pretty Reckless, and many more, inking deals with Koch, Famous/Sony Red/Pavement, and a developmental deal with Capitol Records. Working with legendary platinum producer & Interscope Records co-founder Beau Hill, Tommy Lee, and Will Hunt from Evanescence, Norman Matthew has scored two Top 10 videos on Scuzz TV in Europe, chart debuted at #19 on CMJ, had multiple songs in soundtracks, entrance music written for a professional wrestler (also making his wrestling Wrestlemania weekend 2015), and landed two songs on the ever popular video game Rock Band. Norman Matthew is the founder of the music school and August development studio, The Sound Foundation, in Dallas, established 2012. The first single for his solo project, "Waves," by As Strange As Angels, has been nominated for an Independent Music Award in 2017.

Steven Memel: Internationally Acclaimed Voice Technique and Performance Coach

Steven is an internationally recognized voice technique and performance coach as well as an award-winning actor and director based in Los Angeles. In addition, Backstage voted Steven Memel LA's #1 Vocal Coach two out of the last three years. Creator behind "The Science of Switching On," he has a unique and impactful system that enables him to achieve rapid and dramatic results with all performers. He has aided in building the careers of some of the most talented and successful people in the world of entertainment. Among those who have worked with Steven are recording artists Adam Levine, Sara Bareilles, Halsey, and actors Drew Barrymore, Justin Long, and many more.

PERFORMING ARTIST PATHWAY

Heather Morgan: Nashville Singer and Multi-Hit Songwriter

Heather is a country music singer-songwriter from Richardson, Texas. After graduating from TCU, Heather signed her first publishing deal with Warner Chappell Music. Her songs have been featured on the TV show *Nashville* and recorded by Keith Urban, Brett Eldredge, Sara Evans, Eli Young Band, and Maddie and Tae, to name a few. She is now a staff writer at Sony ATV Music, and had her first #1 single in June 2014 with Brett Eldredge's "Beat of the Music" and was then awarded 2015 BMI Song of the Year. In 2015, she was nominated for Music Row's Breakthrough Songwriter of the Year Award. Be sure to check out Heather's new record, dropping at the end of 2017!

Adam Pickrell: Multi-Record Producer, Music Director, and Keys for Nelly Furtado

Based in Dallas, Adam has been well established in the music industry for nearly two decades, and the last few years have seen his name land on a variety of major-label releases as a musician, producer, and mix engineer. His work has appeared on recordings for St. Vincent, John Congleton, Nelly Furtado, and Cas Haley, among many others. Pickrell works out of his personal studio, Analog Ranch, which houses a collection of some of the industry's most sought-after vintage keyboards, analog synthesizers, and organs, along with some of the most current digital technologies available.

HELP ME, HELP YOU!

my sincere *thanks!*

Thank you so very much for reading my book
Performing Artist Pathway. I hope you enjoyed it!

I need your input to make my next version better.
Please help me out by leaving a REVIEW on Amazon
to give me your feedback! I appreciate it!

With Gratitude,

Brianna

SELF-PUBLISHING
SCHOOL

NOW IT'S YOUR TURN

Discover the EXACT 3-step blueprint you need to become a bestselling author in 3 months.

Self-Publishing School helped me, and now I want them to help you with this FREE WEBINAR!

Even if you're busy, bad at writing, or don't know where to start, you CAN write a bestseller and build your best life.

With tools and experience across a variety of niches and professions, Self-Publishing School is the only resource you need to take your book to the finish line!

DON'T WAIT

Watch this FREE WEBINAR now,
and Say "YES" to becoming a bestseller:

bit.ly/2y6rmOa

RESOURCES

http://briannaruelasmusic.com/contact/

http://stevenmemel.com

http://www.jasonfaunt.com

http://adampickrell.com/sessions--studio.html#about

http://www.normanmatthew.com/biography.html

https://www.thesoundfoundationdallas.com

http://www.culture-hype.com/

http://www.alchemymusictx.com

https://heathermorganmusic.com

http://tiffanyforsberg.com

http://www.firestarterentertainment.com/

http://www.oprah.com/omagazine/oprah-interviews-charlize-theron/all

http://www.dictionary.com/browse/popular-music?s=ts

https://www.livescience.com/39373-left-brain-right-brain-myth.html

http://blog.sonicbids.com/15-unexpectedly-awesome-side-jobs-for-working-musicians

https://irealpro.com

Les Miserables by Victor Hugo

Annie Lennox Quotes. (n.d.). BrainyQuote.com. Retrieved October 12, 2017, from BrainyQuote.com Web site: https://www.brainyquote.com/quotes/quotes/a/anniele nno574509.html

George Bernard Shaw's play, *Man and Superman*

Valerie Young's *The Secret Thoughts of Successful Women: Why Capable People Suffer From the Imposter Syndrome and How to Thrive in Spite of It.*

Psalm 139:14 (NSV Bible)

http://ew.com/article/2000/03/22/why-steven-soderbergh-turned-down-julia-roberts-role/

The One Year Book of Inspiration for Girlfriends . . . Juggling Not-So-Perfect, Often-Crazy, But Gloriously Real Lives by Ellen Miller

https://blog.hootsuite.com/social-media-statistics-for-social-media-managers/

http://www.musicnotes.com/blog/2015/07/16/lead-sheets/

http://www.vocalbrilliance.com/vocal-hygiene-part-2-hydrate-hydrate-hydrate-why-hydration-is-important-to-singing/

http://www.rcttheatre.com

http://deanstreetsociety.com

http://www.vhrestaurant.com

http://everymomstory.com

https://www.cynthiadelorenzi.com

15867663R00115

Made in the USA
Middletown, DE
22 November 2018